Fag Hags, Divas and Moms:

The Legacy of Straight Women in the AIDS Community

Victoria Noe

King Company Publishing

First edition March 2019

Cover design by Jamie Leo
Cover photograph courtesy of Nanette Kazaoka
Interior design by Ladey Adey, Pink Parties Press

ISBN 978-0-990-3081-9-5 (paperback)
ISBN 978-0-988-4632-9-5 (e-book)

Published by King Company Publishing, Chicago, IL

www.victorianoe.com

Contents

Dedication

*To the women in this book and the
thousands whose stories have yet to be told:
all of them inspiring, all of them important.*

*And to my mother, MaryAn J. Noe,
who always believed I could do it, no matter what 'it' was.*

Fag Hags, Divas and Moms

Preface

*"Sometimes you choose your calling
...and sometimes your calling chooses you."* [1]

April 1, 2014

*T*he auditorium at the New York Public Library on Fifth Avenue was filling up, mostly with men. Some were college students from The New School, classmates of my daughter, working on a joint project with the artist organization Visual AIDS. Many were a generation or two older. There were men I knew from ACT UP (The AIDS Coalition to Unleash Power), like Peter Staley and Jim Eigo. David France, whose documentary *How to Survive a Plague* was an Academy Award nominee in 2013, sat in front of us.

We had gathered for a panel discussion, "The Women of ACT UP/NY: Fight Back! Fight AIDS!" held in conjunction with the library's exhibit *Why We Fight: Remembering AIDS Activism.* The deceptively small exhibit, curated by Jason Baumann, was packed with archival material from the early years of protests. Since the exhibit opened in October 2013, the library had presented a series of related events. This one, held the final week of the exhibit, was not originally on the schedule. But there was an oversight to be addressed.

Terri Wilder is the Director of HIV/AIDS Education and Training at the Spencer Cox Center for Health and works with PHAG (Prevention of HIV Action Group) a committee from ACT

UP/NY. She looks much too young to have spent almost thirty years volunteering and working in the AIDS community. She's all too familiar with the ownership of the epidemic: most discussions are dominated by white, gay male voices. So, when fellow ACT UP member Mateo Rodriguez was speaking at the "How We ACT UP" program at the library, Wilder realized that women's stories had been left out of the programming. She approached Baumann and told him she wanted the women of ACT UP to be included. And so, they were.

"The Women of ACT UP/NY" (l-r)
Jean Carlomusto, Sarah Schulman, Terri Wilder
(photo courtesy of Annette Guadino)

The program that night began with a story from Wilder. In 2007, back home in Georgia to finish her master's degree in Social Work, she received an email from a friend she'd lost touch with since the 1990s. During a long, catch-up phone call, she found out that the surprise email had a purpose: her friend had tested positive for HIV. She had made contact after finding AIDS-related articles online written by Wilder.

> As soon as we hung up, I began to cry. I cried off and on for a month over the news. She almost died because they couldn't figure out what was wrong with her. Nobody thought to test her for HIV. I blamed myself for her acquiring HIV. I thought that if I had stayed in contact with her through the years, this would have never happened. [2]

The library panel of seven women, led by Sarah Schulman, writer and co-director of the ACT UP Oral History Project, was a mix of accomplished straight women and lesbians:

- Terry McGovern, Esq. founded the HIV Law Project in 1989 and served as lead counsel on litigation challenging the Federal government's use of a narrow AIDS definition that discriminated against women and low-income people.

- Maxine Wolfe is a founder of the ACT UP/NY Women's Caucus and National ACT UP Women's Committee, as well as Lesbian Avengers and the NYC Dyke March.

- Joan P. Gibbs is a veteran lawyer and activist with many groups, including ACT UP.

- Filmmaker Jean Carlomusto began documenting the AIDS crisis in 1986 as a volunteer for Gay Men's Health Crisis, then with ACT UP. Her current video work, revisiting the early days of the epidemic includes an acclaimed HBO documentary on ACT UP co-founder Larry Kramer.

- Heidi Dorow is an early member of ACT UP, active in women's issues and co-creator of ACT UP's 1988 Gay and Lesbian Freedom Ride, when members traveled through the American South with panels of the AIDS Quilt in an educational crusade.

- Karin Timor was a founding member of the insurance and healthcare access committee of ACT UP/NY.

- Patricia Navarro is the mother of ACT UP member Ray Navarro who died of AIDS complications in 1990. She became a passionate advocate for preventive education and other services in the community. Both she and her son are featured in David France's *How to Survive a Plague*.

The women spoke of their prominent roles in the epidemic. Gibbs talked about the stigma of the early days, when there was no legal recourse for discrimination. Wolfe recounted the story of the four-year campaign to change the definition of AIDS to include illnesses that were specific to women. Dorow described her work with the 'Day of Desperation' protests that paralyzed Manhattan in January of 1991.

I knew most of the stories already. But I'd never heard them told by the women who had lived them. The stories were new to many in the audience, unaware of the involvement of women during the early years of the epidemic. The stories were definitely new to my 19-year-old daughter. Lesbians had always been given well-deserved credit for their contributions. But that evening I realized that I wasn't the only straight woman who had shared the experiences of those women onstage. There were many more of us.

And a thought popped into my head:

These stories need to be told.

Well, not by me, of course. I dismissed that idea out of hand. I knew there were hundreds of books already written about the epidemic, and more in the works. Surely those volumes included the achievements of famous straight women like Elizabeth Taylor and Princess Diana, as well as thousands upon thousands of other women around the world, people on the front lines of the epidemic since day one. Someone must have told these stories already, I presumed.

I spent the next year looking for that book. I searched in libraries and bookstores and online. I asked men and women in the community.

Nothing.

How could that be? I broadened my search to women's history in general, confident that something as important as an epidemic that has killed over 35 million people around the world, half of them women, would include the role of prominent women in the battle. I came across a definitive study of women's history in the second half of the 20th century. But even this offered only one token paragraph about AIDS. It did not even credit the women responsible, women who had been seated onstage that night.

Clearly, there was a gap. Not just in the literature of the epidemic, but in accounts of women's history as well. That left me with two questions: Did anyone care? And was I the person to write the book?

In the fall of 2015, I decided to test the waters. I put out a call on Facebook - on my personal page, my author page, and in the groups I belong to that focus on HIV and AIDS. "I'm thinking about writing a book about the contributions of straight women in the AIDS community. Do you know anyone I should research or interview?"

Within five minutes, my phone was chiming with private messages and texts. Men and women I knew – and some I only knew online – were offering a deluge of names, emails and phone numbers of women to include in the book I had not yet committed to write.

Suggestions came from activists, filmmakers, non-profit executives, artists, academics and medical professionals from across the US, the UK and South America. They shared my question on their own social media pages or within their organizations, so now new messages were coming in from friends of friends.

They wanted to share stories of women who were largely unknown, but whose influence affected thousands. They wanted me to share their achievements, to belatedly give these women the respect and recognition they deserved.

That month, for the first time since I lobbied on the Hill for the Ryan White Care Act in 1990, I attended a major AIDS conference. The US Conference on AIDS was held in Washington just a few weeks after my announcement on Facebook. I spent much of my time with other members of ACT UP/NY, which I'd joined in 2013. Between sessions, I passed out homemade postcards describing what had now surely become my book project. Again, the response was swift and positive:

"Honey, you're writing about me!"

"How many women do you want to interview? I can get you ten at least."

"You can do your book launch at my bookstore."

"When can our magazine print an excerpt from the book?"

This response wasn't what I expected. These were leaders in the community, men and women I'd respected for years. Even strangers were enthusiastic. The support overwhelmed me.

After four days of keynote speeches, networking, catching up with friends and sessions on the state of the epidemic, particularly in the South, I was exhausted. My doubts had been erased. I was now committed to writing this book - though by then it felt more like a surrender.

The final day of the conference, Sunday morning, I attended a rousing gospel brunch. Since many delegates had already checked out of the hotel, I sat with a group of people I didn't know. As the musical presentation began, I watched people dance between tables and sing along. I wondered where they got so much energy. My brain was so saturated with faces, names and statistics that I almost missed what one of the three ministers onstage said during his invocation:

"Sometimes you choose your calling, and sometimes your calling chooses you."

My head jerked up. I felt a shiver through my whole body. And in that moment, I finally understood what I was about to do, what I had been selected to do.

These stories need to be told.

But first I had to tell my own.

"You'll never get a date now."

I'd just told a former boyfriend that I was taking a break from my fundraising consulting practice to become development director at Chicago House and Social Service Agency, a residential program for people living with AIDS. He was right: nothing ruined the evening like telling a guy where I worked. And that was his response.

It was 1989, an odd time to be a straight, single woman. I'd been knowledgeable about AIDS almost since the beginning. There was no question in my mind that everyone was at risk. When I slept with a man, I insisted we use a condom, no exceptions. That decision was not greeted with enthusiasm, even by men I knew had had dozens of partners. Straight men just didn't believe they were at risk. "What do you think is wrong with me?" they'd ask. "I don't know. That's why you're using a condom."

Years later when I saw the 2013 film *Dallas Buyers Club*, I felt vindicated. Finally, almost thirty years later, this film introduced us to the man who co-founded the original club. Ron Woodroof was a straight man with AIDS. He wasn't a hemophiliac like Ryan White. He was infected through heterosexual, unprotected sex. I wanted to call up those anti-condom men from my past and say "See? That could've been you."

While writer and activist Larry Kramer has rightfully described AIDS as a plague, it has always felt more to me like a never-ending state of war. The battlefields were not isolated towns or deserts on the other side of the world; they were densely populated neighborhoods, idyllic suburbs and rural communities. And though it brought false comfort to many to believe the epidemic was not close by and not likely to affect them, AIDS has always been a virus that was too stupid to discriminate.

The decade of the 1980s was a bad time for a new, mysterious virus to appear. The election of Ronald Reagan brought conservatives to power in the US, mirroring what was happening in other countries, including the UK, France and Sweden.

This right-wing wave was a clear reaction to the widespread progressive changes in society during the 1960s and 1970s.

Social conservatives invoked the Bible to justify oppressive new policies that any semblance of humanity. AIDS hospice programs received grants, but funding was denied for condom distribution or clean needle exchanges programs, with politicians boldly citing opposition to what they called deviant lifestyles. Though caring for the sick and dying was in keeping with their beliefs, in their minds AIDS remained divine retribution for sinful behavior.

President Reagan remained publicly silent on the issue - except for cracking jokes - and was unwilling to help a community his constituents found disgusting. Only US Surgeon General C. Everett Koop saw AIDS as a health crisis demanding attention and had live-saving information mailed to every household in America. Still, it was an uphill battle for those trying to raise awareness and funding, as they were facing off with people who believed anyone infected deserved what they got. People who professed to follow God's words, who usually preached compassion, wanted my friends dead.

The first time I remember being conscious of AIDS was March 1983. My girlfriend was in the hospital after a difficult labor and delivery that called for a transfusion. When I visited her there, her skin was whiter than her sheets. She worked in the lab at that hospital and knew the blood supply hadn't been carefully screened and wasn't safe. Eventually she agreed to the transfusion and suffered no complications.

I was volunteering occasionally, taking on grant-writing assignments from AIDS organizations until I took a job at Chicago House in 1989. My boss admitted that it was not his decision to hire me, that he wanted a gay man in that position. I was the only straight person in the office. I watched gay co-workers fawn over other straight women to their faces and ridicule them behind their backs. Every part of their lives was fair game for attack: hairdo, makeup, weight, taste in men. Even their motives for involvement in an AIDS organization were questioned.

It was in that working environment that I was called a 'breeder' for the first time. I'd never heard that expression before I started working in the AIDS community. Until then, the only hostile label had been 'fag hag'. The animosity surprised me.

Anonymous notes were left in my desk and in my mail slot, one indicating disgust at my alleged bad breath. My boss went through my file cabinet and then left a memo with detailed descriptions of faults in my record-keeping. One infraction cited was that I had attached a sheet of correspondence to the right-hand side rather than left-hand side of the file folder.

At first, I was confused. Then hurt. Finally, I was angry. I had no agenda. I just wanted to do my job and help.

I came from a theater background, so I'd had gay friends since high school. But I've never been to a college reunion because it would've been too painful; too many of my male classmates had died from AIDS. I found out one of them, David Aurand, had died when I saw his panel on the cover of a book about the NAMES Project AIDS Memorial Quilt.

The work at Chicago House was challenging and exhilarating and sometimes frustrating. The mission statement read: "Chicago House and Social Service Agency provides residential and support services for people living with HIV & AIDS." The problem, as it turned out, was the word 'people' - everyone assumed we only served men.

So, I did something that was, well, wrong. I didn't ask permission, and I certainly had no right to do it, but I changed that word in the mission statement for my grant proposals. I changed 'people' to 'men and women'. With that text change, it was as if a light bulb went on: the reaction from potential funders was markedly different. "You have *women* living there?" And just like that, new funding came into Chicago House.

We maintained a full calendar of fundraisers: regular events at Little Jim's (a gay bar that banned women, excluding me from my own events) and Roscoe's (a gay bar where I was welcome), drag shows, a dunk tank at Halsted Street Days, and our first black-tie event at the Drake Hotel.

I was in London at a theater in the West End on the first World AIDS Day, December 1, 1988. At the curtain call for *The Secret of Sherlock Holmes*, Jeremy Brett made a speech appealing for support. The ushers passed around buckets to collect donations to support local AIDS service organizations. I stole that idea the following year, and we sent volunteers to theaters to collect money for Chicago House. And though my boss was not enthusiastic, the volunteer coordinator was. He continued and expanded the event.

The fact that I was straight and female was sometimes an advantage. I could attend corporate events and meet with people who were open to giving money as long as they didn't have to actually come into contact with anyone HIV-positive (i.e., gay men). And though I wanted to scream at them, I kept my mouth shut because I wanted their donations.

I was good at my job: I could raise $1 million a year back when that was a huge amount of money. I saw other straight women volunteering and attending fundraising events. Their interior designer or stylist had died; maybe a nephew or a son. Their grief drove them, just as it drove the gay men who started AIDS-service organizations at their kitchen tables, because no one else would help their friends.

After a year, my position was eliminated and I left Chicago House. My post was replaced with a job description that only a handful of experienced fundraising professionals in the area were qualified to fill. The job still required overseeing events, writing foundation and government grants and individual donor campaigns. Now it included something that was typically a separate specialty: capital campaigns. It was not a surprise when that new job went to a young, attractive, less-experienced white gay man. I continued to raise money in the AIDS community as a consultant with groups like Bonaventure House and Stop AIDS until 1994.

Meanwhile, ACT UP was making its mark as a direct-action organization. I was too busy raising money to take to the streets, so I watched ACT UP protests from a distance. I admired their passion, though I didn't always agree with their tactics. More than once I felt they went a step too far. But at least they were doing something. As the epidemic raged on, the casualties rose. And I was not spared.

Victoria Noe and Steve
Showalter, Chicago House
Gala, Sept 15, 1990

About two years after I became a consultant, I hit a stretch of eleven weeks in a row when someone I knew died. All were men I'd known around the community, had worked with on projects, or just knew socially. But one loss really hurt: Steve Showalter had been my assistant at Chicago House. He was 28. I had actually objected to Steve being hired: he had AIDS and I needed an assistant who could do the literal heavy lifting. And though there were times I had to be mindful of his health, he was the best co-worker anyone could have. He was kind and fun and willing to learn. We made a good team.

When I heard about the eleventh death, I knew I had to get away, as far away as I could. It was unrealistic to believe I could run away from the epidemic. But I had to at least get away from Chicago. I called my former acting teacher Mike Genovese in L.A., whose home was always welcome to visitors. and asked if he had room for me. As soon as he said yes, I booked a seat on Amtrak. That meant two days with no phones, and no contact with others unless I wanted it. Two days of staring out the window at mountains and desert, listening to Phil Collins' *No Jacket Required* in an endless repeat on my Walkman. By the time I arrived, I was able to hold a coherent conversation. Reconnecting with him and his wife, having dinner at the Chinese-Peruvian restaurant on Colorado Boulevard, and just sitting on the front porch restored me. By the time I came back to Chicago a week later, I was rested enough that I could work again.

I bought a copy of *And the Band Played* On, Randy Shilts' indictment of pretty much everyone involved in the early days of the epidemic. I remember very clearly throwing the book across my living room several times. I would read about government inaction, or medical fraud, or politics, and I'd have to stop to throw the book. My best friend once asked why I read such a history when I'd already lived through it. The anger: that's why. In 2012, at the Smithsonian Folkways Festival, Gert McMullin from the NAMES Project told me that anger fueled her involvement. It fueled mine, too.

Now and then, I'd mention to a friend that I was going to a memorial service. Or that I was visiting someone on the AIDS ward at Illinois Masonic Hospital. Or that I'd referred someone to Herdegen-Brieske (the only Chicago funeral home that would handle bodies of those who died of AIDS). Their response would often be: "How did they get it?" There were few things – then or since – that could instantly infuriate me like that question. My responses were not exactly polite; the nicest I could come up with was "What the hell difference does it make? They're dead."

Looking back on that time, I was angry a lot. I felt as if I was living in London during the Blitz: never knowing where the bombs would drop, only that someone I knew would die. And most people didn't give a damn.

In 1993, I married John Chikow, a man who welcomed my gay friends. He had to - it was non-negotiable. A nonprofit consultant after 16 years working for the Boy Scouts, John had a lot to learn about my world. But my friends quickly became his friends. Our wedding flowers all had red ribbons, and our reception was held in the Gold Coast Room at the Drake Hotel, the location of the first Chicago House charity gala. One of my former volunteers designed my invitation; another sang at the wedding. During the ceremony, we remembered those lost to AIDS.

My father wanted our first dance to be Bette Midler's "Wind Beneath My Wings" but for the first time in my life, I refused to do something he asked. I couldn't do it, I told him, because virtually every memorial service I'd ever been to included that song. It was just too sad for me. So, we danced to "Sunrise Sunset" from *Fiddler on the Roof*. Twelve years later, "Wind Beneath My Wings" was the only song played at Daddy's funeral.

When our daughter, Emma, was born in 1994, my priorities shifted. We brought home this tiny, beautiful baby a few days before my 42nd birthday. Marriage and children had seemed unlikely just a few years earlier. She would be our only child, so I wanted to concentrate my time and energy on helping her grow into the smart, kind, creative young woman she is today. And frankly, I was burned out. I kept up with the medical advances and marked World AIDS Day. But otherwise AIDS faded into the background.

I changed careers, selling books to Chicago Public Schools and conducting book fairs for the next fifteen years. While my daughter grew up, my career was working with librarians and teachers. I enjoyed it.

On St. Patrick's Day 2009, I had a minor fender bender but suffered a concussion. I struggled for months to maintain my sales career, but post-concussive syndrome put an end to it. Quite unexpectedly, it opened a new door: writing.

Back in 2006, I told my friend Delle Chatman about an idea for a book: stories of people grieving the death of a friend. Though I'd never written a book before, Delle, always supportive, encouraged me to do it. What followed were several attempts to start the book, yet they always stalled. When Delle herself died a few months after that conversation, I suddenly and ironically found inspiration from my own grief. But it wasn't until I was recuperating from my concussion in 2009 that I was finally able to begin to keep that promise to Delle to move forward on the book.

I've known and admired Tracy Baim, veteran publisher of *Windy City Times*, Chicago's LGBT newspaper, since the late 1980s. In 2011, she asked me to write a reflection on my time in the community for her "AIDS at 30" series. I agreed, though reluctantly - I wasn't sure I could remember anything from that dark, frightening time.

I was wrong.

I sat down at my computer and typed whatever popped into my head about that time. Slow to start, I soon began typing faster, the heartbreaking, chaotic memories flooding back. The keyboard fairly smoked, but what scared me was how quickly the anger surged. While I may have been out of the community for a long time, the epidemic had left its mark on me.

I decided to break up the book into a series of small books. Each would be about grieving friends who died in different situations such as 9/11, the military and the workplace. But I always knew one would be about AIDS. I visited the AIDS Quilt, on display again on the Washington Mall during the Smithsonian Folkways Festival in 2012 and spoke with some of the founders. I caught up on the current state of the epidemic, both here and abroad. I saw the documentaries *United in Anger* and *How to Survive A Plague*, nodding in recognition like a bobble-head doll when I wasn't crying. By the time I published *Friend Grief and AIDS: Thirty Years of Burying Our Friends* in March 2013, the anger was simmering once again.

That April, I walked into my first ACT UP/NY meeting at the LGBT Community Center on West 13th Street. I was surprised to see a group of only a dozen or so, not the overflow crowds of the early days, as depicted in documentaries. I sat in back at first, not sure of protocol, but was quickly waved into the circle by veteran activist Jim Eigo. He announced that he'd be in West Hollywood later that month for a benefit screening of *How to Survive a Plague*. As luck would have it, I was also scheduled to be in LA for a conference and book signing. We met up again at the benefit, along with William Lucas Walker, who took some of the most iconic photos of Peter Staley and others at early ACT UP/NY demonstrations. In June, I met Peter at a World Science Festival program held at the New-York Historical Society, in conjunction with their "AIDS in

New York: The First Five Years" exhibition.

It was on that trip to Los Angeles that I had dinner with Trudy Ring, a volunteer when I was on staff at Chicago House and now a writer for the *Advocate*. We'd reconnected, as many do, on Facebook. Over Thai food in Westwood, we shared stories of our experiences as straight women, including our time in the same office. And I realized for the first time, that I'd cut myself off from an important support system: other straight women in the AIDS community.

I'd felt so terribly alone. It never occurred to me to band together with them - Trudy was not the only one. I knew other straight women: staff, volunteers, board members at dozens of agencies in Chicago and California. But I hadn't reached out. I had self-isolated, convincing myself that it was self-care. And that was a decision I still regret.

During those dark years of fundraising events, memorial services, meetings and hospital visits, I did not make one straight female friend in the AIDS community. And I paid the consequences. I wasn't just alone. I was lonely. I cut myself off emotionally because I simply didn't believe – until Trudy proved me wrong – that any of them shared the same experiences.

Talking to women outside the community was useless. They couldn't understand why I was working there in the first place, much less what I was going through. My mother's first comment upon reading the book was, "I had no idea you were going through that. Why didn't you say something?" People I'd known for twenty years were surprised to learn of my involvement.

Straight women have entered the AIDS community throughout the epidemic for various reasons, but all with the same intent: to make a difference. Some were comfortable, some most definitely were not. Whether it was the challenge of researching a frightening new virus, ensuring that no one lose their jobs or homes because they were dying, or just the determination to support a friend or loved one, they – like me – wanted to help.

I was asked at one of my first ACT UP meetings why I was there. My immediate response: "Because I've never been arrested and I think I'm way overdue."

It was a flippant comment. But I never imagined that the epidemic would still be an issue in the 21st century. Nor did I expect that the contributions of straight women around the world would still be ignored – not just in the AIDS community, but in accounts of women's history as well. It's time for straight women to come out of the closet.

These stories need to be told.

Introduction

Now is the time to reach out. Now is the time to see that every man and woman is allowed to live in dignity, a dignity we maintain by sharing our joys, our sorrow, our passions, and our love.
Now is the time to care for each other and ourselves.
- Colleen Dewhurst [1]

Acclaimed actress Colleen Dewhurst was known for her performances of strong, independent women. Whether it was as the classic leading ladies of Shakespeare and O'Neill onstage, or as Murphy Brown's mother, the characters she brought to life were forces of nature: confident, aware and determined, much like Dewhurst herself.

So, it was a surprise that she fell prey to the same lack of awareness that afflicted so many people in the early days of the AIDS epidemic.

> *You Can't Take It With You* opened [on Broadway] in April of 1983, a time that many people, myself included, were first hearing about AIDS. I didn't think I knew anyone who had come down with this mysteriously fatal illness. Now I know that I did, but my denial fed their fearful silence and that silence created an atmosphere where even people like me could comfortably think of AIDS as something very far away. [2]

One cast member, Orrin Reilly, understudied the young leading man. He and fellow actor Jimmy Coco frequently went out for Japanese food with Dewhurst to gossip about the rest of the cast.

Colleen Dewhurst, Equity Fights
AIDS Flea Market, Sept., 1990
(photo courtesy of Broadway Cares/
Equity Fights AIDS)

Always full of energy, he soon tired easily and sometimes missed performances, reportedly because of mono or a case of pneumonia. Through these growing absences, Dewhurst clung to her denial.

The day finally came when Reilly called Dewhurst at home. It was time to tell her the truth: that he had AIDS. The news shattered the actress' denial, but not her love for him. She went to his side immediately.

> Short of holding his hand, I didn't know what to do. But that day I woke up. Someone I loved had AIDS. How many more would there be? How long would other well-meaning people be able to remain as numb to this as I had been? [3]

Other straight women around the world would experience similar awakenings: the diagnosis of a friend, a family member, a coworker. Sometimes their own infection was the awakening.

The women in this book were not, are not, silent, though they may have started out that way. Some were friends and colleagues of gay men. They worked in professions where gay men were prominent: performing and visual arts, design, fashion. Whether comfortable with their friends' sexuality or not, they worked side by side. Gay men were their neighbors, teachers, students, hair stylist. They were patients, clients and colleagues.

For most people today, it's difficult to understand the abject fear and paranoia of the early days of AIDS. But the era was one of misinformation and mystery over scientific fact. There were few facts that we could point to as absolute. It was infectious, but was it contagious, too? What if your waiter had AIDS? Could you get it from vaginal sex, sharing food or eating utensils? What about a kiss, a sneeze or a handshake? In the fourth decade of the epidemic, these fears appear silly. But the 2017 "HIV in Ireland" survey found that globally erroneous notions have not disappeared:

> One in five 18 to 24-year olds incorrectly thought HIV can be passed from person to person through the sharing of a public toilet seat, compared to 10% of those over 24.

> 24% of people incorrectly believed that HIV can be transmitted through kissing, while 11% wrongly thought it could be transmitted through coughing or sneezing. [4]

Though these respondents are in a minority, the fact that these results came in 2017, not 1987, is hardly cause for celebration. Nor are the findings unique to Ireland.

The epidemic of the 1980s meant healthy young men wasted away in months or weeks from infections so rare that few doctors had ever seen them before. Most were diagnosed only after the virus had decimated their immune systems and left them vulnerable to opportunistic infections. This confounded the medical establishment and terrified the general public. Assuming that only gay men were affected, health officials pushed abstinence as the only solution. Gay bathhouses were threatened with closure and some voluntarily shuttered their doors. But it soon became clear that unprotected sex was not the only means of transmission. When AIDS cases became known among hemophiliacs, babies and heterosexual adults, many finally took notice of the epidemic.

Those with AIDS were divided into camps: guilty and innocent.

Gay men always fell in the first category. They were getting the punishment they deserved as sinners, so proclaimed self-righteous religious leaders. Intravenous drug users and sex workers soon joined them in this category. There was only one resolution: repent in order to be saved. They'd still die a horrible death, of course, but at least they'd be spared eternal damnation.

The second category included babies born to mothers with AIDS. Media called them innocent victims, making the moral point that all the others deserved their illness. Their mothers, however, were judged by how they were infected. If they were infected by husbands who had cheated on them or were IV drug users, they were absolved. But if the women were sex workers or drug users, even single mothers, well then, they deserved it. And they were often deemed unfit to care for their children.

"Women Don't Gets AIDS. They Just Die From It", Gran Fury Collection (Image: New York Public Library)

For many years, HIV-positive women were acknowledged only in terms of their child-bearing ability. They became part of the conversation when they were pregnant, with the focus on their child's health. Even after women were finally considered for HIV drug clinical trials, they were often excluded based on their future potential for childbearing. Drug testing and treatment options were based on the experiences of white, gay men. Women's hormones were considered a disqualifying complication. Incredibly, they still are.

These were the battle lines drawn in the first years of the epidemic. Straight women entering the community as staff or volunteers soon discovered that agencies were fragmented, serving specific populations, often with limited functions. Some focused on delivering meals or providing legal advice. Others provided emergency housing or free testing. Few served gay men and children, or gay men and straight women, or a diverse ethnic base. And while some of those distinctions were appropriate and more effective, a choice had to be made.

Caring for those affected became a perverse game of selective morality. Which group do you support? Whose side are you on? Do you align yourself with the group that is the least objectionable - babies - or do you stand up for the others and risk a unique guilt by association? Do you instead find a third-party, such as a church or corporate volunteer program, in order to keep a distance while still being involved?

The straight women in this book are not the only ones who have made a contribution over the course of the epidemic. Each represents thousands of women around the world who have not yet told their stories, whose dedication to supporting those with the virus and preventing others from being infected has never been truly honored.

Of course, not every straight woman hurried to the side of a person who had just been diagnosed. First, they had to process the information and the equally shocking revelation that the person was gay, an IV drug user, or a sex worker. Some women initially rejected the infected. Only after facing down their own fears, would they come around. Some never did. To imply that all straight women rushed in with nonjudgmental support is to ignore the damage done by women like First Lady Nancy Reagan.

On July 24,1985, actor Rock Hudson's publicist sent a telegram to Hudson's long-time friends in the White House. He was stricken with AIDS and his doctor believed the only hospital in the world that could treat him was a military hospital in Clarmont, France. Hudson was initially refused admittance, but the doctor believed an intervention from the Reagans would change the situation. Mrs. Reagan declined to use the power of the White House to save their friend, although her husband did phone Hudson to express their sympathies.

The reason given by the Reagans, with obvious political calculation, was that it would be unfair to help a Hollywood friend with a favor they would not bestow on anyone else. The truth was that conservative Republicans condemned liberal Hollywood, despite the irony of a movie star - and former liberal - in the Oval Office. Like her husband, Nancy Reagan remained silent on the epidemic. In 1987, long after Hudson had died, amfAR co-founder, Elizabeth Taylor urged the First Lady to get involved in the AIDS community. The official response was, in the words of Taylor's amfAR co-founder Dr. Mathilde Krim, "frosty." Eventually Taylor shamed the Reagans into appearing at an amfAR event on May 31, 1987, where for the first and only time, seven years into the epidemic, the president finally uttered the word 'AIDS.'

When Elizabeth Dole assumed the leadership of the American Red Cross in 1991, it was an agency under siege. Poor response to natural disasters had taken a toll, but nothing like the fire storm at Congressional hearings that called into question the safety of the nation's blood supply. For years, the Red Cross had resisted government safety regulations, resulting in lax practices about blood screening. Therefore, HIV-tainted blood was being distributed unknowingly, causing needless infections and avoidable deaths.

Initially, Dole's dedication to the job included convincing qualified experts to join the agency. She expanded the board of directors with people who had decades of business experience and

*First Lady Nancy Reagan and
Elizabeth Dole, luncheon for Senate
spouses, Blue Room, White House,
June 14, 1988*

a willingness to donate large sums of money. To the public, things were looking up.

Behind closed doors, it was a different story. Dole gathered a special team of advisors around her. They weren't staff or board members. They had no legitimate power but served as a buffer between Dole and the outside world, and within the organization as well. Their purpose, as staff soon realized, was to direct the Red Cross with politics in mind.

Her husband, Senator Robert Dole, was running for president, and this special team vetted all the organization's policies with two goals. First, would it generate good public relations? Second, could they curry favor with the right-wing Conservative Christians that Senator Dole sought for support? AIDS was a problem.

AIDS education was part of the Red Cross's mission: accurate, appropriate information for all ages. They went into schools and the workplace. Not bound by any particular ideology, they offered balanced, science-based programming and materials. While abstinence was stressed, so was the importance of clean needles for IV-drug users, proper use of condoms and regular testing. They received well-deserved credit for their independence, at a time when this was sorely needed.

The Catholic Church aggressively opposed the use of condoms not only for contraception but for prevention of HIV transmission. The Christian right - particularly in the South - was enjoying success around the country by ensuring that abstinence-only sex education be taught. In the spring of 1995, the Red Cross AIDS Manual was being updated. It was a routine process, necessary in the days when treatments were changing, that didn't warrant senior-level involvement. But Dole's special team got hold of it. For the first time, the staff was directed to fundamentally change the agency's information on safe sex.

Previously objective and science-based, the Red Cross was now committed to the conservative political belief in 'personal responsibility.' Often used to justify draconian cuts to social welfare programs, it was now being used to defend abstinence as the only true way to avoid being infected with the virus. The use of condoms was downplayed as a sign of support with the Catholic Church.

By 2008, Dole was no longer at the Red Cross. Her husband had retired, and she was now a senator from North Carolina. Though many in the AIDS community did not support then-president George W. Bush, they do give him credit for one thing: PEPFAR. The President's Emergency Plan for AIDS Relief, first enacted to strong bipartisan support in 2003, provides over 11 million people with antiretroviral drugs in 60 countries. Successes include over two million babies born HIV-negative to mothers with HIV. New infections have plummeted almost 76% in some African countries. It remains a success story in the global fight against HIV and AIDS.

One senator especially hostile to people with AIDS was Jesse Helms of North Carolina. He despised homosexuals, believed AIDS was punishment for a sinful lifestyle, and voted against AIDS funding time and again. In turn, he was despised by the national AIDS community for repeatedly impeding progress in HIV research and treatments.

But two weeks after Helms' 2008 death, Elizabeth Dole, who now held his senate seat, accorded the AIDS-phobic politician a posthumous honor. She added a last-minute amendment to the PEPFAR legislation to name it in Helms's honor. It was an entirely symbolic gesture because she filed the amendment too late to be considered. Still, she was publicly on record as playing to hers base by trying to honor a man who spent decades spewing hatred against anyone and everyone with AIDS.

Indifference or outright opposition by straight women was not limited to the early days of the epidemic. As late as 2017, a Georgia state representative, Dr. Betty Price (an anesthesiologist married to former Health and Human Services Secretary Tom Price) inquired at a public hearing about the legality of quarantining HIV patients to stop the spread of AIDS. After all, she added, people with AIDS were living longer these days, thereby posing a greater risk of spreading the virus. She later issued a statement insisting that her comments were taken out of context.

Make no mistake: those who remained silent caused as much damage as those whose vocal histrionics condemned people living with HIV and AIDS. Perhaps it was simply a human response, the fear of the unknown. This was, after all, a mysterious and deadly virus that no one could cure, that seemed to attack those at the margins of society (with the occasional celebrity for good measure). The result of that silence, the unwillingness to overcome fear and prejudice to search for a solution, proved deadly. The stigma attached to HIV and AIDS - even to this day - has kept the end of the epidemic just out of reach. As ACT UP continues to remind us, Silence=Death.

Friendships between gay men and straight women have frequently been the subject of ridicule. The term 'fag hag' - denoting a straight woman who associates with gay men - was never meant as a compliment. But perhaps because both groups had long known discrimination, a bond developed. There was a comfort level on both sides. Until the dawn of the AIDS epidemic, the friendships between straight women and gay men happened behind the scenes, not centerstage. Straight women did not typically take a public stand to support causes that affected the health of their friends. That is, until HIV/AIDS brought many of those friendships out of the closet.

The 1970s altered that dynamic. It was an era of radical change. Gay men and women found common ground. The Gay Liberation movement, birthed at the Stonewall Riots in 1969, paralleled the women's movement in many ways. There was no thought of marriage equality in the LGBT community then. But ending legal discrimination based on marital status, sexual orientation and gender, as well as celebrating personal sexual freedom became goals of both movements.

It has been widely acknowledged that straight women and lesbians with roots in those movements were integral to early organizing efforts around HIV/AIDS. Their experiences with legislative advocacy, direct action and grassroots organizing helped groups like Women's Health Action and Mobilization (WHAM!) and the AIDS Coalition to Unleash Power (ACT UP) grow in size and power quickly.

Cynthia O'Neal, founder of Friends in Deed, describes what many straight women discovered, especially in the early days of the epidemic:

> ...we talked about the fact that tragedy can transform people in amazing and wondrous ways, and how what I have observed in the gay community - the way people are taking care of one another, the fact that I have seen people who are so very ill themselves take care of a friend or lover who is even more ill than they - is as inspiring and beautiful as anything I have ever seen. There is a lot of heartbreak - there is also a lot of love. [5]

But almost four decades into the epidemic, white gay men still tend to be the face of HIV/AIDS. In documentaries, memoirs and public discussions, they are the default spokespeople. To be fair, the first AIDS-focused organizations were founded by white gay men. Initial advocacy efforts were led by white gay men. The first celebrities identified as people with AIDS were white gay men. Straight women are still mostly invisible, a galling fact because they remain at great risk for infection, especially women of color. Their contributions to research, care, advocacy, awareness and education have been lost, both in and out of the HIV/AIDS community.

Jih-Fei Cheng, Assistant Professor in the Feminist, Gender and Sexuality Studies Department of Scripps College, studied how AIDS has been portrayed in popular culture. He found that even David France's Academy Award-nominated documentary *How to Survive a Plague*, chronicling the early days of ACT UP, failed to chronicle diversity in the AIDS community:

> To describe the absence of women and people of color in *How to Survive* as being 'stark' is not to proclaim that they are merely invisible and/or deceased. Rather, their absence is marked indelibly and excessively. [6]

Whether it's the race to put a man in space or the creation of Tiffany lamps, women's roles have been erased or ignored. The AIDS community is no different in that regard. Some of the women on the following pages are famous. Most are not. But their commitment to supporting those who are HIV-positive and their efforts towards ending the epidemic deserve recognition.

Fag Hags, Divas and Moms

The Volunteers

*"I have known several people afflicted with AIDS,
some of whom have died, and I would like to be of service."
- Joan Tisch, from her application to volunteer at
Gay Men's Health Crisis.*[1]

Nonprofit organizations, including AIDS service organizations, rely heavily on volunteers. Today's huge nonprofits, like GMHC (formerly known as the Gay Men's Health Crisis) and others, did not start off with paid staff and office space. They were born around kitchen tables, over coffee at a local diner, or late at night in a neighborhood bar. They were born of desperation to meet overwhelming need. Sometimes armed only with an idea and the desire to do something, the groups started with people eager to donate their time and money and energy to addressing the epidemic.

Women showed up at these new, passionate and often loosely structured organizations to help out in any way they could. Many of them were in unfamiliar territory, not just thrust into the LGBT community, but in close contact with people with AIDS. Some were close to a friend, a colleague, a family member who had AIDS, or someone who had already died. Some volunteered as a way to thank that organization for their support of that person. Others had no idea how they could help. They just wanted to.

Nothing says "straight woman volunteer" like the Junior League. While traditionally viewed as merely white-gloved, upper-class, elitist white women, the organization has a far more interesting history.

Founded in 1910 by Mary Harriman, daughter of financier Averill Harriman, the initial group was called The Junior League for the Promotion of Settlement Movements. These ten young debutantes were inspired by the work of Jane Addams at Chicago's Hull House, instrumental in assimilating immigrants. They determined to raise money for an initiative called The College Settlement, where college students and graduates would live among immigrants to learn about their needs. Harriman believed that privileged young women like herself had the opportunity – and obligation - to leverage their exalted positions in society to improve the lives of a vulnerable population. The idea caught on - eighty more women joined The Junior League the first year.

Issues impacting women and children have always been at the forefront of The Association of Junior Leagues International (AJLI). Their current service projects focus on issues such as human trafficking, environmental advocacy, domestic violence, career development and since 1986, AIDS. Their mission is now shared by over 150,000 women in 291 Leagues in four countries. Their most famous members include Eleanor Roosevelt, Sandra Day O'Connor, Eudora Welty and Shirley Temple Black.

In 2016, Martha Strayer was honored with the Mary Harriman Award, AJLI's lifetime achievement award. Her Junior League experience began in Erie, Pennsylvania. An early, passionate environmentalist, she confronted Hammermill Paper Company about their waste disposal system, which had ruptured in 1968, causing a noxious black plume to seep into an abandoned gas well in Presque Isle State Park. In 1974, now in Toronto, she was asked to serve as Junior League of Toronto's representative on the board of Planned Parenthood, helping establish a youth health clinic that disseminated birth control information, which had just become legal. In 1988, she became a founding director of Fife House.

Housing programs for people with HIV, typically found in large, old houses or apartment buildings, began to spring up around the country in 1985. Often referred to as 'supportive housing', they were structured to provide more than just physical shelter. Residents were supervised by on-site managers who coordinated staff and volunteers to ensure that their needs were met. Whether it was transportation to doctor appointments, communal meals, therapy or social outings, these houses became the most nurturing homes many HIV-infected people had ever known.

Fife House, the first housing program in Toronto, opened in 1990, serving five people with HIV/AIDS. Now operating five sites, it provides 80% of the supportive housing services in that city. Adjusting to the demands of the epidemic, its services now also address the needs of older people with HIV whose health is complicated by cognitive and other aging issues.

Russel's accomplishments are impressive, but they represent a fraction of the organization's involvement in the AIDS epidemic.

In every League, members sign up for projects that can be one-time only events ("Done in a Day") or year-long commitments. Echoing the group's original mission, many projects focused on the impact of HIV/AIDS on women and children. But they soon expanded beyond that.

In 1986, the Junior League of Los Angeles became the pioneering group committed to projects within the AIDS community, establishing the AIDS Community Education Outreach Project in partnership with AIDS Project L.A. (APLA). They staffed a hotline and began a corporate speaker's bureau. Subsequent projects included coordinating the volunteer program for Caring for Babies with AIDS and co-sponsoring Ask Us About AIDS with Culver City Youth Center, a peer counseling program for at-risk adolescents in that city. Eventually, sixty other Leagues would establish their own AIDS projects.

As early as 1987, The Junior League of San Francisco was working with two established nonprofits organizations: The Shanti Project, founded in 1974 to support people with life-threatening diseases including AIDS through peer support programs, and Home Care & Hospice Project (a project of JLSF, Visiting Nurses and Hospice of San Francisco).

One of the new wave of Junior League members who maintained

busy careers, Susan Gatten was first confronted with the epidemic when a colleague at Charles Schwab died from AIDS in 1982. She was responsible for convincing the JLSF to award a $35,000 grant to Shanti, the first large donation they'd received from a non-gay group. And while that was a good start, Gatten wanted the League of do more. "Our city," she wrote as president to the members, "has never faced a more formidable foe. More San Franciscans have already died of AIDS than were killed in the Great Earthquake of 1906."

Junior League members and resident,
AIDS Homecare and Hospice Program, 1989
(photo courtesy of Junior League of San Francisco)

Gatten understood the unique position of the women in Junior League by creating a speakers' bureau that could influence the corporate community in ways the gay community could not. The chapter faced down community opposition to open Hope House, a halfway house for women with HIV who had been formerly incarcerated. And through their work with Shanti, helped dispel misconceptions about Junior Leaguers and change their own beliefs about the gay community.

In April 1987, Gatten used her position as president of JLSF to introduce a resolution at the Association of Junior Leagues international conference, calling on its 170,000 members to get involved in AIDS work.

In 1988, the provisional class (first year members) of the Junior League of Montclair-Newark, NJ took on a project involving infants. At that time, Newark had the highest number of pediatric AIDS cases in New Jersey. The women adopted Babyland IV, a daycare center for children with HIV, aged three months to three years. The class renovated the center, providing fundraising, caregiving and administrative support for the children and their parents.

Recognizing that volunteers needed information to fight the epidemic, AJLI began publishing the "AIDS Network" in 1989. Sent to every Junior League chapter, the newsletter shared resources, conferences, training programs and funding possibilities, along with articles that informed, educated and corrected myths.

Each individual league sends out regular correspondence to their members. AIDS was the special focus of the January 1989, issue of "Fogcutter" sent to the San Francisco league. One-third of the issue was devoted to updates on current projects, legislation and education. But perhaps most heart-breaking was an anonymous essay written by one of the JLSF sustainers (a member who has achieved a 'retired' status).

In it she relates the fear and shame she experienced when her husband was diagnosed with AIDS. The pain of his excruciating decline was matched only by the shame and determination to keep his secret. Most of their family and friends did not know the truth. Like many LGBT partners, she did battle with insurance companies and faced off against family members who refused to visit while her husband was alive, showing up only after his memorial service for their expected inheritance. At the end of her essay she begged for compassion and offered to speak to anyone who had questions. But even among friends, she was unwilling to identify herself.

Also, in 1989, the Junior League of Mexico City developed an AIDS education component for all of its existing projects (Project LEAD, Woman to Woman, Alcohol and Drug Awareness and the Women's Health Clinic) that served youth, women and parents. Their involvement began when they were approached by

CONASIDA (National Committee for AIDS) to partner with them and the Secretaria de Salud (Secretary of Health). The League members were trained in AIDS education and prevention and eventually created Mexico's first AIDS information forum, working in health clinics and public schools.

That same year, the Junior League of Annapolis helped create a Teen Pregnancy/AIDS prevention project and convened the AIDS Task Force Coalition in Anne Arundel County, a coalition that included local health, education and social service offices as well as YWCA, Annapolis Gay People, Jaycees, American Red Cross and more.

Throughout the country in the early days of the epidemic, Junior Leagues provided hands-on service in a variety of ways. In addition to educating themselves, they created AIDS awareness and educational programs in communities such as Honolulu, Sarasota, North Little Rock and Tyler, TX.

Their involvement was not only defined by direct service or fundraising. The structure of AJLI and individual Junior Leagues includes an active public policy committee, identifying issues of importance to women and children on the local, state and federal level and pro-actively advocating for them.

Many 'outside' organizations stepped back from partnering with AIDS organizations in the late 1990s. And though their projects have dwindled now to a few, Junior Leagues continue to support the AIDS community.

When Trudy Ring decided to volunteer at Chicago House in 1988, she considered herself one of the second wave of volunteers: people who did not have a personal connection to AIDS, but because of their social circles, believed it would hit home soon. She wasn't sure what she wanted to do, what she could contribute. But she was very clear on what she didn't want to do: she didn't want to work in one of the agency's homes for people with AIDS. It wasn't a lack of commitment, but rather a realization that the emotional toll would be too much for her.

She was content to show up in the office to stuff envelopes and help with fundraising events, enjoying the camaraderie with other volunteers, some of whom were living with AIDS themselves. It proved the advice she received from the volunteer coordinator, Ernest Tripp: volunteering can't be all about altruism. He advocated for building relationships, making friends, learning skills. In other words, getting something out of it. Ernest was an energetic, witty man whose approach to volunteering convinced Trudy to devote the next four years to Chicago House.

*Trudy Ring and Ernest Tripp, Chicago
House Gala, Sept. 15, 1990*

Ring's desire to protect herself emotionally, however, did not last. She made friendships with gay men who were HIV-positive, including Ernest: friendships that lasted until they died.

During the early days of the AIDS epidemic, women of a certain elevated social status were expected to limit their activity to writing checks and serving on the boards of select non-controversial nonprofits. Described as GMHC's 'most famous anonymous volunteer' in a 2011 profile by Marjorie J. Hill, billionaire Joan Tisch began her involvement in 1986, content to answer phones, stuff envelopes and help clients decipher medical bills. She was first and foremost, willing to do whatever was needed, without public recognition or title. Tisch was eventually asked to serve on GMHC's board of directors, and later made substantial donations that enabled the organization to acquire expanded office space.

Terri Wilder has made AIDS her life's work. Her career began as a volunteer in her native Georgia. Just after graduating from the University of Georgia, in the summer of 1989, she saw a pink, tri-fold brochure advertising an "AIDS 101: Action and Awareness" workshop. Though it had not been addressed in her coursework, she figured this would enhance her career as a social worker. Still, she was reluctant to go alone, and recruited her father to accompany her.

The day-long workshop covered all aspects of the epidemic from education to prevention that gave her the facts she needed for her prospective clients. The final session was a recruiting pitch, outlining various volunteer opportunities: AIDS hotline, outreach, social support. The one that piqued her interest most was a buddy program.

Buddy programs popped up in 1982. Healthy volunteers were paired one-on-one with a person with AIDS. They provided practical and emotional support - often the only support. The programs typically were offered through LGBT and AIDS service organizations in cities like New York, San Francisco, and Chicago. They relied on referrals from health care and social service professionals who identified patients in need. Wilder thought it was perfect for her.

It took a long time for her to get a placement; most of the clients were gay men who wanted a gay man as a buddy. Finally, she was matched with a gay man who didn't care about his helper's gender. The relationship was challenging but worked for a while, though eventually they lost touch. Without a placement, Wilder moved up in the volunteer ranks to take over the role of buddy captain.

As a young woman now intent on a career in the AIDS community as a case manager or social worker, Wilder still felt the same pressures as any single, straight woman. Family members simply kept asking why she wasn't dating a man.

Gradually, Wilder recognized the second-class status she faced in the AIDS community, observing, "Sexism isn't always obvious."

How many times do you go to a lecture and the lecturers are men, or white men. Or if there is a woman up there, they talk over her or don't give her a chance to talk.

Do I see it now? Is it the reason I don't go to ACT UP meetings? Absolutely. [2]

One way to become a volunteer in the AIDS community is to join a shared activity. AIDS Walks, held in dozens of cities around the world, draw teams of walkers from hospitals, pharmaceutical companies, churches and synagogues, schools, banks, restaurants and bars. These events are not unlike other walks and runs that raise money for less controversial diseases: breast cancer, ALS, juvenile diabetes and Alzheimer's. They did not require actual contact with people with AIDS, and that distance was often important: participants could say they took a stand - without getting too close to those infected.

In the early days of the epidemic, straight women served as a bridge between the AIDS community (assumed to be wholly gay) and the world. Like the Junior League, they often began with projects benefiting women, particularly those with children, avoiding the controversy of being associated with a gay cause. For some, that was as far as they could dive into the community, comfortable knowing they were helping 'innocent' victims.

It's easy to look at these women through the prism of the 21st century and criticize them for half-hearted support of the community. But for the first 15 years of the epidemic, participants risked guilt by association. It was a powerful deterrent to participation. And not just for straight women; closeted gay men donated money anonymously, wanting to support the cause but unwilling to go public about it. Straight men stayed even farther away.

Those early days were terrifying and not everyone had the emotional strength to get involved. But for those who did, the rewards included knowing that you made a profound difference in the lives of infected people. In addition, these heroic efforts transformed the volunteers themselves, in countless ways.

And as veteran AIDS activist Terri Wilder would observe years later, "Volunteers are activists whether they call themselves that or not." [3]

The Educators

"Secrets keep you sick." - Sarah Thomas [1]

When the AIDS epidemic began, and was thought to be restricted among gay men, education took a very narrow form. Posters in bars and bathhouses were typical ways of educating gay men on safe sex techniques, complemented by free condoms. "How to Have Sex in an Epidemic", a sexual guide written by HIV-positive New Yorkers Michael Callen (a cabaret singer) and Richard Berkowitz (a hustler) in 1982, was widely distributed and remains a classic. Medical professionals, many unaccustomed to conversations about gay sex, were trained by those on the front lines. The Denver Principles, a manifesto written by a cadre of infected gay men, demanded that patients be proactive partners in their care, educating and even challenging their doctors and caregivers.

Women, particularly straight women, were often not allowed in gay bars, and certainly not bathhouses. But they took advantage of their gender - and the assumption that they were medically 'safe', unlike gay men - to expand educational efforts. It was here where cultural and racial differences challenged the entire AIDS community.

Most AIDS service organizations were started by white gay men to serve white gay men. They understood their clients who were just like them. When it became obvious that the face of AIDS included women, particularly women of color, the original policies no longer worked.

Education wasn't just about the slogan "use a condom every time," although that continues to be the default advice. It had to include a host of other interconnected matters: affordable health care, fact-based education, housing insecurity, domestic violence, spirituality, misogyny, drug addiction, homophobia, child care and jobs. Handing out free condoms did not help women in a community that expected them to obey their husbands, where females did not have the authority to demand that men wear a condom. It would not help in a community in which churches condemned women to hell for doing anything that prevented pregnancy. For these women, AIDS was just one more strike against them in a life marked by abuse and disempowerment. They were not going to leave their kids with a neighbor after dinner so they could ride 100 blocks on the subway to a downtown office building for a presentation on safe sex. And they certainly were not going to sit and be lectured to by white women who had no concept of how they lived their lives.

That meant women, especially women of color, had to find new ways to educate communities at risk, ways that had to be culturally appropriate in order to be effective. They achieved it by focusing on educating and enlightening women: teenage girls, adult women, mothers, grandmothers.

Rosa E. Martinez-Colón has been an integral part of the AIDS community in Chicago since the mid-1990s. Like many, her earliest memory is of whispering and shame. In 1984, she was still living in Puerto Rico when she learned a neighborhood friend died after a short stay in the hospital. The rumor spread rapidly that the man, an injection drug user, had "died of AIDS" – "se murió de SIDA". Soon after, a couple other neighbors died as well; they had been either a sexual partner or drug buddy of the drug user. "I did not pay much attention to it," Martinez-Colon later recalled. "It did not concern me at that time." [2]

In 1993, studying at Northeastern University in Chicago, Martinez-Colón was asked by a classmate to help find meeting space for a group connected to the AIDS community. Her business loft had plenty of room, so she agreed.

It will sound weird to say that I miss those days. After all, back then most of our hours were spent with hospital visits or making funeral arrangements. That part I don't miss at all. But I do miss the camaraderie of those days. I miss the fact that back then we were one force together fighting against a common enemy.

Back then for two hours on Saturdays we all gathered at our space, females, males, gay, straight, injection drug users, old and young, and spoke about the challenges of those living with HIV/AIDS and those of us doing our best to help. There were many tears shed, but also a lot of laughter, a lot of happy moments. There was food, music and celebrations. [3]

Martinez-Colón's turning point was the realization that education and support efforts were not culturally appropriate on the most basic level: materials were offered in English only. She became heavily involved with C.A.L.O.R. (Comprehensión y Apoyo a Latinos en Oposición al Retrovirus). But her main focus was serving women in the community.

CALOR at Chicago AIDS Walk, 1993
(photo courtesy of Rosa E. Martinez-Colón)

To that effect, we started a weekly support group for women only. And to make sure that they were able to participate without worrying about their children, we also had an activity group for the kids. So, while their mothers were in the group, discussing issues that were pertinent to them and the HIV status, the children were in another room engaged in other activities. *(4)*

In 2009, Karyn Brianne Lee and Luvvie Ajayi were bloggers based in Chicago. Ajaji always wanted to have a red shoe ball for Africa, an elaborate party where women wore gorgeous red shoes - red being the color most associated with AIDS - because someone she knew had cousins orphaned by the epidemic in Africa. With National Women & Girls HIV Awareness Day approaching, they suddenly had a Mickey & Judy moment: "Let's put on a blogathon!"

Bloggers typically write an essay, post it on their blog and walk away. In a blogathon, after a post is published, the blogger remains online to answer questions and comments from their followers. They may even add additional posts. But it requires a time commitment that is unusual. Lee and Ajayi had hoped to sign up a couple dozen bloggers. Within ten days 130 people were committed.

After a wildly successful first event, the two women hosted a meetup night with bloggers. Though this was originally approached as a one-time project, the conversation among eager participants proved that there was sufficient interest in making this an ongoing campaign.

Here was an opportunity to connect with other women, particularly women of color, in a setting other than sterile lectures. It was a teachable moment that neither woman wanted to waste. They held a fundraiser to benefit Chicago Women's AIDS Project and by the end of the year became a 501(c)3 nonprofit. They expected to simply raise money for established organizations. But eventually they realized that they could reach African-American women that other organizations could not. They needed to start their own nonprofit. So, the Red Pump Project was born, "to educate women and girls of color about HIV through bold programming and digital initiatives."

They quickly established several successful annual fundraisers - Rock the Red Show (a fashion show in Chicago during March), The Red Summer Soiree (held in Washington DC in June), and The Red Pump/Red Tie Affair (in Charlotte, NC, to mark World AIDS Day). The Red Pump Project soon became known nationally for offering a unique educational and entertaining presentation for women.

Eventually reaching their target audience in 19 cities, Cupcakes and Condoms® paired a dessert table of red velvet cupcakes with a concise, informative and entertaining overview of HIV/AIDS education for African-American women. Information was disseminated about PrEP (Pre-Exposure Prophylaxis), proper use of condoms - including the female condom - was demonstrated, attendees were directed how to discuss safe sex with your partner, and also were directed on how to access local health services. The event became an effective way to target a demographic often overlooked.

The Red Pump Project focused on cities that are not New York, San Francisco or Los Angeles. They targeted cities with at-risk African-American populations and spearheaded outreach to women, a demographic where HIV continues to climb.

One underserved group Red Pump targeted were faith communities. Stigma in black churches has been a significant barrier to effective outreach. They first reached out to pastors' wives. The reasoning: even if they themselves are not HIV-positive, these women knew people in their congregations or families or neighborhoods who were infected.

As a straight woman, Lee had encountered little pushback from family and friends in her HIV educational efforts. In fact, her willingness to take a stand was applauded. Her husband came from the deep South and understood the access challenges addressed in both her volunteer work and career. As Marketing Manager (Special Pharmacy) for Walgreens, she leads communication strategies designed to raise the profile or their over 700 HIV-specialized pharmacies.

Educating women helps Lee resolve her greatest frustration: "Why aren't more people talking about this?" She realized that the structural challenges in the black community - access, jobs, housing, etc. - make it harder to reach people. But her efforts surmounted these barriers. When she reached infected or at-risk people with lifesaving information, it became her greatest joy.

She welcomed women who found community through Red Pump. In 2012, one woman told her she got her friends involved supporting the organization, without telling them she herself was HIV-positive.

In July 2018, Lee and Ajayi made the difficult decision to shut down The Red Pump Project. And while there was great sadness at the loss of such a unique organization, the two women have demonstrated that their priorities continue to remain in the right place:

> We've grown up while stomping around in our red shoes. And it is such a part of us. It's something we cherish. It has been a true honor to lead Red Pump and to have served alongside so many incredible women in our journey.

> We have always been a vessel of knowledge but each of you holds the true keys to help move our mission and this greater cause forward. Thank YOU to everyone who has supported us over the years. We could not have done this without you.

> While we are closing the chapter on Red Pump, we will never say goodbye to the cause that birthed this organization. If HIV affects one of us, it affects all of us. We look forward to using our gifts and talents to advocate for this important issue in many other ways. [5]

Do not look to the women's movement for leadership when it comes to HIV/AIDS. You won't find it. Historians who document the women's movement of the 20th century have little if anything to say about women's health beyond reproductive rights, and next to nothing about their leadership in fighting HIV.

Do not look to public or private educational institutions for leadership in HIV prevention. "Abstinence only" government-mandated sex education programs ignore the facts about HIV.

Do not look to religious institutions in the battle to curtail HIV infection. They refused to overcome centuries of misogyny to embrace practices that help women make informed decisions about their own bodies.

Do not look to the medical establishment, led by government institutions like the Centers for Disease Control. It took the government until 1992 to revise the definition of HIV/AIDS to include the unique ways the virus presented itself in women. Until then, many were discouraged from testing in the belief that the anxiety would outweigh the likelihood of an HIV-positive diagnosis. Access to clinical trials continues to be limited by researchers who lament the 'complication' of women's hormones. Even today, women are not offered HIV tests by most American doctors because their risk is perceived to be miniscule.

Copyright NYC Dept. of Health & Mental Hygiene, reprinted with permission

Where does that leave straight women who are HIV-positive? They are already in a minority in the US, though worldwide 51% of AIDS cases are female. Some pioneering women start organizations to help others like themselves. Some go to work for organizations, using their experiences as powerful teaching tools to reach at-risk communities. And some tell their stories publicly, stepping out of their self-imposed closet in the hopes that they can save a life.

Many point to a system that has consistently failed them. They cite a lack of accurate, stigma-free sex education as a factor in their ignorance about HIV. Heather Arculeo grew up on a farm in Kansas. There, talk of sex was so taboo that parental permission was required for a student to take an anatomy class in high school.

A self-described 'All-American Girl', Arculeo enlisted in the Marine Corps after graduation, serving as a firefighter. Two brief marriages, both producing a daughter, followed. Then, finally, she found happiness in her third marriage. So, her HIV diagnosis came as a shock.

> "I did not understand how this diagnosis was possible," she said. In fact, she laughed when her CO informed her that her regular blood donation had tested positive for HIV. "I was married, had children, didn't do drugs and was definitely not sleeping around. This was far from the stereotype I had of individuals living with HIV and AIDS." [6]

With only a month to go before her 2007 discharge from the Marines, Arculeo was immediately enrolled in a two-week class at Balboa to help her adjust to her diagnosis. She was the only woman. Even after she left the service and went to the VA Hospital in LaJolla, she was still the only woman in the room. For five years she felt completely alone, until she happened to see a flyer advertising a women's retreat at Christie's Place, the only nonprofit in San Diego County whose mission focuses on women, children and families impacted by HIV/AIDS. She immediately felt a sense of belonging.

"This was the first time that I became aware of the possibility that I may not be alone in this journey," she thought. (7)

The majority of the women at the retreat, she found, shattered stubborn and inaccurate stereotypes of drug users and sex workers. Like her, they'd been infected by their spouses or boyfriends. Though her husband initially denied he was HIV-positive, she learned the truth eight years later.

The Christie's Place retreat was the starting point of Arculeo's new life. Armed with knowledge and surrounded by a supportive community, she pledged to set an example, to both educate women about HIV and empower them. As she tells others, "Change is possible even if the transformation seems impossible."

Growing up in southern California, Kelly Gluckman believed HIV/AIDS was something that happened to other people: gay men, IV drug users, Africans. Still, even after she moved in with her boyfriend, she insisted on practicing safe sex, using a condom every time...until she didn't. A competitive gymnast when she was growing up, she was sensitive to changes in her body. So, after feeling a shift in her well-being, she went to Planned Parenthood with her boyfriend to be tested for HIV. Both were sure the results would be negative.

They were both infected. While her boyfriend insisted he hadn't cheated on her, Kelly eventually learned the truth: he'd had unprotected sex with at least a dozen men.

At first Kelly was in denial. She believed incorrectly that Magic Johnson had been cured of AIDS. Even when she accepted her diagnosis, it wasn't enough to get her on medication. But after her viral load tripled in three months, she finally started on a treatment regimen. At first her drugs came from the Ryan White Care Program, because she didn't want her parents to find out from their insurance company (She was still covered by the family policy).

It took time for Kelly to get accustomed to her new life as a woman with HIV. But she slowly and steadily took control of her life. She started by breaking up with her boyfriend. Then she revealed her

Kelly Gluckman and Thomas Davis of
Black AIDS Institute, World AIDS Day
2018 educational program
(photo courtesy of Kelly Gluckman)

diagnosis to her family and close friends. By that time, Kelly also realized she was not living with a death sentence. She also realized that she had a story to tell - not just the story of a young straight women with HIV. She could teach young people how to protect themselves in a sex-positive way. Soft-spoken and determined, Kelly went public. She became involved in an advertising campaign "Let's Stop AIDS Together" and then appeared in "I'm Positive," a 2013 MTV documentary. The next leap forward was joining the UCLA Sex Squad, a performing arts troupe that tours high school to share sex education. Her passion for education also led her to be named an ambassador for the Elizabeth Taylor AIDS Foundation, her work focusing on youth outreach. A colleague at ETAF praised her efforts, explaining,

> "Kelly's openness to tell her story has been invaluable for furthering [our] mission to see an end to the HIV/AIDS epidemic...Every time Kelly shares her story, she is helping to remove the stigma that surrounds HIV." [8]

Martha Cameron is a lifelong advocate for women in girls. In 2003 in her native Zambia, she became the director of Every Orphan's Hope Ministries. Not all of their clients were HIV-positive, but all had been affected by the epidemic, as tight-knit families had been disrupted with the death of a parent who was the breadwinner. That work gave her purpose, because Martha had recently been diagnosed with AIDS. By 2009 she married an American who'd come to Zambia on a mission project and moved to the US. They had two children, who, along with her husband, are HIV-negative.

Cameron continued her involvement. After completing a master's degree in public health and a fellowship with UNAIDS. she joined the Women's Collective. A leading non-profit organization in Washington, DC, it was founded by Patricia Nalls in 1990. An HIV-positive woman herself, Nalls wanted to combat the isolation she felt by offering appropriate services to women, girls and their families impacted by AIDS. Cameron, now also an ambassador for the Elizabeth Glaser Pediatric AIDS Foundation, is acutely aware of the challenges in educating women in the American South:

> The death rates in the South are highest among women living with HIV. It blows my mind that here in a country where you have some of the best healthcare systems in the world, there are people suffering because they can't access it or afford it. As an immigrant, it humbles me that the trauma and issues faced by African-American women here are comparable to African women where I come from. [9]

Nancy Duncan, of Valley Stream, NY, was not unaware of the AIDS epidemic, but because her ex-husband was healthy, there seemed no reason to get tested. After all, in 1990, there was no cure and treatment options were limited. Why bother?

But when Nancy found out she was HIV-positive in the fall of that year, she was ashamed, embarrassed and isolated on Long Island, far from Greenwich Village, the epicenter of the epidemic in New York City. The distance was more than geographic - AIDS awareness was squelched in her area and services were modest.

It wasn't until six months later that Nancy was visited by a caseworker from Long Island Association for AIDS Care. She was referred to a support group at a synagogue in Rockville Center, and as other women have found, she was the only HIV-positive woman in the group. But the shared experiences and challenges made her a little less alone for the first time.

Within a year, the group welcomed more women. She was never judgmental about the gay community and she felt accepted. But as much as these support groups helped Duncan and others, she always felt a Damocles Sword hanging over the meetings.

> People would come and go, get sick and many passed away. I felt like I didn't want to get close anymore and feel the hurt of losing them. Seeing them in their last days before they passed was very hard, and always in the back of my mind was 'When is this going to happen to me? Will I be so emaciated and ill also?' I did almost succumb to the complications of AIDS several times in those years. Having support helped me get through it and I guess it just wasn't my time. [10]

Support on Long Island continued to be hit and miss. The larger, more established AIDS service organizations were in Manhattan. Their services were superior, but required long, expensive commutes to the Village, midtown or Harlem. Efforts to rotate locations to accommodate people like Duncan were unsuccessful.

Looking after her young son occupied Nancy's time, as did a bout with cancer in 1994, It was a challenging time for both of them, as she recalls.

> My son was only 10 when I learned I was HIV-positive. I chose not to tell him right away because I felt he was too young to understand. But after two years of hospitalizations, sickness and quitting my job as a letter carrier, he asked me what was going on. I knew I had to tell him then and it broke my heart to have to do this. He cried when I told him and asked questions I couldn't answer. He didn't want anyone to know because he was afraid no one would want to be his friend. He had been doing

so well in school and not long after he started to do poorly, and he also started to gain weight. He saw horrible things happen to me mentally and physically, especially in 1996 when I also had lymphoma, that no child should have to see his mom go through. (11)

In 1997, with the release of the HAART cocktail, Nancy and fellow group members were thriving. She felt and looked better and now believed she would live to see her son turn 18. And though she wasn't healthy enough to go off of Social Security Disability, she wanted to give back.

Nancy joined a speaker's bureau at LIAAC. At community events, she shared her story of how a newly-divorced woman had unprotected sex in 1985 with a guy who didn't know he was HIV-positive. The ordinary circumstances of her transmission defied stereotypes of who got HIV and how. In 2004, she took a job at Planned Parenthood of Nassau County (NY) as a peer educator.

It was more convenient for Nancy to watch the efforts of activists from afar. By 2012, however, she raised her level of engagement and began joining AIDS-specific Facebook groups, including ACT UP/NY. Soon she was going into Manhattan to participate in town halls and demonstrations.

Like many straight women with HIV, Nancy found dating to be less than satisfying. She tried online dating sites for people with HIV and dated one HIV-positive man for ten years. But a visit to a comedy show at the church down the street from her home reacquainted her with a friend from high school.

Howie is my boyfriend. We've been together for about six years. I met him in 1974 when we were teens hanging out in the local park. We were both dating other people at the time. I then ran into him through a mutual friend in 2011. I told him I was HIV-positive but had no intention of dating him. I had never dated an HIV-negative man since my diagnosis in 1990. He asked my friend for my phone number about a month later. I was hesitant to call him because I was still afraid to date a negative man and I told him that. We hung out as friends for about six months and he asked if we could take the relationship further. I loved him and wanted to be with him, so I told him I'd give it a try. He has never shown any fear of me at all and we use condoms always and that is a mutual decision. He lives with me now and we get along okay, but sometimes I don't think he understands what it's like living with this for so long and the constant fatigue I have. [12]

Nancy is still working for Planned Parenthood, staffing their street outreach van, offering pre- and post-test counseling, and connecting with women to empower them about their personal health decisions. Her greatest value, she feels, is to show by example that an HIV diagnosis can happen to anyone.

In stark contrast to Nancy Duncan's suburban Long Island community, the Austin neighborhood on Chicago's west side can be a very bleak place. In many ways it has never recovered from the riots and fires following Martin Luther King's assassination in 1968. It's a frequent re-entry location for recently-released offenders. Although infection rates among inmates is two to three times higher than the general population, it wasn't until 2012 that the state of Illinois mandated HIV testing in their facilities.

In 1995, Angela McLaurin was convicted of drug possession and processed at the Dwight Correctional Center for Women in north central Illinois. During her intake, she was handed a piece of paper listing the risky behaviors that made her vulnerable to HIV. McLaurin had already noticed something wasn't right with her health, months before her arrest. So, while HIV tests were optional at that time, she thought it would be a good idea to be checked.

Imprisonment saved her life. McLaurin was diagnosed with HIV, then fortunate enough to be able to be placed on the new drug cocktail that was saving lives.

As her release approached, McLaurin was determined to get an education. She earned her GED and a bachelor's degree in applied behavioral sciences from National Lewis University.

McLaurin appeared in a 2012 video designed for people in the correctional system, produced by the AIDS Foundation of

Chicago. "Outside the Walls: Life Beyond HIV", was screened for inmates of the Illinois Department of Corrections to encourage them to learn their status and connect with support services after their release. In the video, McLaurin voices a personal philosophy that transformed her into an inspiration for women around the state. Staring into the camera, she said with determination, "I'm a testimony to the fact that there is life beyond HIV. I have HIV; HIV does not have me." [13]

Born into a privileged family, Sarah Thomas moved around the country several times due her father's advertising work, including North Hollywood where Bob Hope was a neighbor. She is outspoken about the risky behaviors - drugs and extramarital affairs - that escalated for a while after high school.

By 1996, Thomas had been clean and sober for nineteen years. She'd also had her suspicions about the possibility of an HIV infection. After donating blood at the Red Cross in Baltimore, Thomas learned that she was HIV-positive.

With the news of her diagnosis, Thomas resolved to take advantage of support networks and adhere to her treatment regimen. Her focus is on her health, as it should be. But it wasn't enough. She decided to speak out, to reveal her past as a way of inspiring others who were too ashamed to speak up. It wasn't easy: it took her six years to share the news with her mother. And two decades before Thomas finally agreed to a public interview with Penn Live, central Pennsylvania's leading local news outlet.

"Based on my upbringing it shouldn't have happened to me. But it did." [14]

What progress has been made in addressing HIV among straight women? It has been a mixed bag. While they have represented no more than 20% of all HIV infections in the US in the history of the epidemic, on a global scale they account for 51% of all cases. The US figures are sharply defined by race, with only about 19% being Caucasian.

Iris De La Cruz,
undated (Iris House)

Iris De La Cruz of New York City was a pioneer among women in the HIV community. During the 1980s, she fought for her life and the lives of women like her, as well as sex workers, when no one was listening to the voices of straight women of color. De La Cruz was often the only woman in the room when AIDS services and policies in NYC were being discussed. But she made sure her voice was heard, because so many depended on her. She inspired tens of thousands before dying in 1991 at age 37.

When you read her poem, "Ode to the Sisterhood", you can hear her voice and feel her anger and determination, even if you never had the privilege of knowing her.

> Here's to all the women
> The nameless, faceless souls
> That died alone
> Warriors
> In combat
> Forgotten
> Beside their brothers.

Here's to Linda
Dead
Who died ashamed of a virus
Trying to gain access
To a drug trial
That might have saved her life.

Here's to Migdalia
Who died
A prisoner of war
Trapped in a fourth floor walk-up
Cold, starving and crippled
Denied of benefits
For the cancer
That ate her womb.

And don't forget Marie
Who spoke no English
And was deemed healthy (and stupid, lazy)
By a callous, asshole social worker
Deaf to the poetry in her native Creole
Who spent her last days
Feeling hopeless and dirty
And alone.

Shaheen died on a stretcher
In a city hospital
From ovarian abscesses
The surgeon refused to operate
(tainted blood. No insurance)
So she drowned in her own pus.

Paula overdosed
While awaiting a bed
For herself and her baby

In a drug treatment facility
She was afraid
Her child would be left an orphan
Not to worry
The kid died, too.

And here's to myself
An aggressive bitch
Who tears at her hair
And shrieks in agony
Every time I lose a sister
I pray that our screams are heard
And our tears fall on your heads
Even from the grave. (15)

After two years of assessment and planning, in 1992 an organization focused on the needs of HIV-positive African-American and Hispanic women opened in East Harlem. De La Cruz did not live long enough to see it become a reality, though her mother, Beverly Rotter, helped. Today, Iris House stands as a tribute to her fierce determination to give a voice to women previously unheard and invisible.

The Nonprofit Executives

"I didn't think I was doing anything special.
I did what anyone would have done under those circumstances."
- Ruth Brinker, Founder, Project Open Hand [1]

In the early days of the epidemic, many AIDS service organizations were started by gay men. Due to widespread homophobia, they realized they would have to care for one another. So, they started housing programs. They opened clinics. They provided legal services. They launched food delivery systems. Arguably the most famous organization is Gay Men's Health Crisis, now known as GMHC.

In 1981, six gay men and their friends gathered in Larry Kramer's living room to discuss a response to the new, frightening 'gay cancer'. Initially focused on raising money for research, they quickly realized that basic services for gay men already facing stigma and discrimination were the most pressing need. Their AIDS hotline, little more than an answering machine in Rodger McFarlane's home, logged over 100 calls the first night from people desperate for information and assistance. In 2017, GMHC served over 13,600 clients, one-quarter of them women. The staff has grown as well, including a number of straight women like Krishna Stone.

Krishna, Director of Community Relations, has been on staff at GMHC since 1992, hired from the ranks of volunteers to recruit buddies in the outlying boroughs. Buddy programs were established to provide one-on-one support for people living with AIDS, and GMHC's was one of the first. She was not the only straight women there, but she was in the minority. Krishna wasn't initially there because of a personal connection. She, like others, was there because "folks are dying and this is really scary". [2]

Krishna Stone, Grand Marshal, 2017
NYC Pride Parade
(photo courtesy of Krishna Stone)

The love of her life, Max, was a waiter at the popular midtown Manhattan disco The Ice Palace. But they broke up when she found out he was having sex with men. They remained friends but eventually lost touch. One day they ran into each other again. She was walking out the door at GMHC and he was walking in: as a client. Krishna became part of Max's caregiving team and remained by his side as he declined. By then she had an infant daughter, so she brought the baby with her to Sloan-Kettering to visit him. Max died in 1995.

(His death) was very, very, very personal. It was really rough. Met him in 1978. Stayed kind of connected but lost track. But he had such an impression on my heart. But being a new parent, couldn't make it to his funeral. I couldn't. [3]

Many AIDS service organizations were started by straight women. Some were driven by that personal connection, others by a near-religious zeal to help. For others, AIDS care was an extension of their current careers. One such woman was Ruth Brinker.

A San Francisco-based retired food-service worker, Brinker recalls her first connection to the epidemic upon the death of a neighbor in 1985. Horrified to discover that malnutrition had been a contributing factor, she enlisted several friends to cook and deliver meals to people with AIDS. That was the beginning of Project Open Hand, the first organization in the US to provide nutrition to people with AIDS. Today there are over 100 organizations around the country continuing the work she began, with many expanding their client base to people with cancer and other life-threatening diseases.

That same year across the country in New York City, a hospice volunteer named Ganga Stone delivered a bag of groceries to a man named Richard. What she found when she arrived shocked her: he was too sick with HIV to get out of bed and the refrigerator was bare. Richard hadn't eaten for two days. He angrily told her he needed a cooked meal, not a bag of food he didn't have the strength to prepare. Stone got him a meal right away, paying for it out of her own pocket. But that was obviously not a long-term solution.

Like Brinker, Stone convinced a group of friends to prepare meals to deliver to homebound people with AIDS. The following year, God's Love We Deliver was incorporated. In its first nine years, they delivered over a quarter million meals.

One might think that medical advances have ensured that people with HIV or AIDS are no longer too sick to cook for themselves. One would be wrong. That these food delivery groups are still needed today is proof that the need has not disappeared. Today, there are over 100 similar organizations around the country.

Susan Rodriguez was a legal secretary in East Harlem in 1995 raising three children. One day she discovered her husband was HIV-positive - and so was she. Unable to find women-focused HIV information, she taught herself about the basics and then shared what she learned with others in the community. In 1998, Susan co-founded Sisterhood Mobilized for AIDS/HIV Research and Treatment (SMART).

SMART takes a holistic approach: a one-stop shopping for all things needed by women affected or impacted by HIV/AIDS. SMART offers testing, education and medical treatment. But they go further, providing other crucial services: safe, affordable housing; legal rights and mental health support; lessons in controlling stress and eating healthy; counsel in escaping domestic abuse and raising resilient children; finishing school, training programs and help in finding jobs. SMART's mission is to address every aspect of the lives of every woman who walks in the door.

In West Harlem, Ingrid Floyd, Executive Director of Iris House, came to the AIDS community in a very different way. After earning an MBA from the University of Pittsburgh Katz Graduate School of Business, she began her career at Deloitte Consulting in New York. HIV and AIDS were definitely not part of her work life. But when she was approached about serving on a nonprofit board of directors, a memorable moment from her freshman year of college guided her choice.

It was 1993 at South Carolina State University. Floyd was listening to a guest speaker, an African-American woman. This woman's sorority had held a blood drive, and naturally she donated, only to have her blood rejected. She was HIV-positive. Until then, Floyd had thought of AIDS as something affecting mainly gay men. The idea that a woman so much like herself could contract the virus convinced Floyd to be tested.

In those days, the wait for results was ten days. Living at home, Floyd rushed each day to retrieve the mail before her mother, so she wouldn't find out. Fortunately, the results came back negative. But that experience made the epidemic personal for the first time. She knew she needed to think about it in a different way.

Floyd traveled a lot for Deloitte, including a stint in India. Whereas AIDS and safe sex were not part of the conversation in New York, India was a different matter. There was much more awareness there than on Wall Street. Floyd knew she wanted to get involved in increasing that awareness, particularly for women of color. After two years on the board of Iris House, and with a desire to make a life change, Floyd left corporate America to join the staff as deputy director.

While on the board, Floyd had an experience that mirrored that of many other straight women. She'd been going to the same gynecologist for years but had never been offered an HIV test. So she asked for one. The nurse gave the test. Floyd explained that she was leaving on vacation, and the nurse said she would only reach out if the results were positive. When her phone rang a few days later, Floyd was shocked. But the nurse informed her the test was negative. Relieved but annoyed, Floyd asked why she had called. "Well, you looked so worried."

The transition from corporate world to nonprofit world is not always an easy one. But Floyd drew on her project management skills to get the organization's programs and finances in order. She was named Executive Director in 2005.

Floyd soon found herself in a position familiar to many straight women who have worked in the AIDS community. Meeting with representatives of other New York City AIDS organizations, she was in the minority. It was difficult to break into a group where everyone else was an expert with two decades of experience. New ideas, particularly new ideas that involved addressing the epidemic among women of color, were not always welcome, Floyd found.

In various meetings, Floyd found that the majority kept the agenda focused on the needs of gay men with HIV. Discussions of the needs of women with HIV were often tabled or aggressively pushed aside. What's more, when she asked for her perspective to be heard, the executive director was often told she didn't understand the issue because she is not gay.

"I do understand because a lot of the issues are the same," she said. "The stigma might be different but it's there. Let's work collaboratively to address all the issues we're dealing with. For every young gay man there's a mother who's concerned. Plenty of straight women get it and want to work on the issues and be part of the solutions. We have to figure out a way to work together." *(4)*

Though it's easier now than it was years ago, there remain challenges to bringing women into conversations about HIV and AIDS. Less money is allocated by government programs and private funders for women's programs. Because of the success of the antiretroviral drug cocktail, the urgency of the first fifteen years of the epidemic has lessened. That results in less coverage in the media. When public awareness is down, complacency reigns. Because of this level of complacency in the mid-90s, women's infections spiked.

"We can't let that happen again," Floyd insisted. And in a statement that's not often publicly declared, she cited one of the greatest challenges to those fighting the epidemic today, and why Iris House expanded their programs: "You can't talk about straight women and AIDS without talking about straight men." *(5)*

Carol D. Marsh founded Miriam's House in 1996 in a seedy, run-down abandoned building on Washington DC's northwest side. She was inspired as a teenager by books like Christy, a historical Christian novel about a young privileged woman in 1912 Asheville, North Carolina, who volunteers to teach needy children in rural eastern Tennessee and learns the challenges of navigating cultural differences. Marsh decided to devote her life to social justice.

Carol D. Marsh, undated

She began her career at Samaritan House in 1990. It was her first job after moving to DC, as a resident manager at their home for homeless pregnant teens. Her white, sheltered suburban self was shocked by the extremes of not just homelessness, but attendant issues such as pregnancy, drug abuse and violence. She'd expected that her willingness to be part of the solution would make her happy, but she was miserable. While still going through orientation, she met with the addictions counselor to complain.

"I don't get it. I'm just trying to help."

Clayton must have had to deal with many 'helpful' women like me. He said what he must have known he was going to say as soon as we'd met. "You ain't trying to help. You're trying to get liked." [6]

It proved to be a lesson she was slow to learn.

Marsh and her husband lived on-site at Miriam's House, in this first home for African-American women with AIDS. All residents struggled with complicating issues such as addiction and homelessness. Marsh's idealistic intentions were soon challenged by something she did not anticipate: that the management skills she'd gained were very different from the skills required to lead a community of vulnerable and damaged women.

Clashes with residents and staff became all too frequent. It was more than just a matter of different communication styles. To Marsh, the other women were a mystery to her.

"I had never felt so different," Marsh recalled. "So white." [7]

In the beginning of the epidemic, the myth that AIDS only affected gay (mostly white) men meant that community-based group created a crisis care model geared exclusively for that demographic. But as the epidemic grew and affected more people, it became clear that the virus did not discriminate based on race, gender or geography. New models of intake and care had to be developed. The arrival of straight women to this scenario meant they were able to develop some of those new models. But that didn't guarantee that the needs of infected women of color, particularly poor women, would be met. The model had to evolve and diversify even further to accommodate the many demographics being affected by this growing scourge.

On one otherwise relaxing Saturday morning, Marsh became the target of one resident's wrath. Any question, even one as benign as "How was your bath?" was met with an angry reply. Marsh tried to remain dispassionate in the face of resident's criticism, but instead began to fear that she wasn't helping anyone by being there. Recalling that conversation with the addiction counselor in 1990, she now understood where she had erred: the residents did not owe her friendship or gratitude. She continued to throw herself into her work, this time with a healthier attitude that did not depend on validation from those she served.

But Carol Marsh, like many, was showing signs of burnout. The demands of being the executive director of an organization that had no real business models was taking a toll. She came to a point where she wasn't sure why she was still there or whether she could stay.

If I tried to talk about how much I loved the women and how difficult their lives had been and how it seemed the right thing to do in this unjust world, I sounded trite and pious, even to my own ears...Yet underneath all the complication was tucked away a rather simple explanation: I simply could not imagine myself living anywhere else or doing anything else. [8]

Her determination was fueled by witnessing the women's struggles with recovery. An area nursing home refused to admit one of her residents because she had AIDS, a condition omitted in the home's existing nondiscrimination policy. Marsh fought back and won a discrimination lawsuit against the nursing home. This type of discrimination was familiar to these African-American women. But it was new to her.

Carol Marsh was not the only straight woman to realize that her continued presence in the AIDS community depended on avoiding burnout. But each had to find their way and assemble a support system that would enable them to continue their work. For many, it's identifying a support system, sometimes within the work environment, sometimes separate. Among the strategies that have helped them continue their work: Learning new skills, finding solace in their faith, connecting with other women, and especially, taking care of themselves.

For nonprofit executives, their involvement in the AIDS community could put a damper on their social lives. When asked where she works by her dates, Krishna Stone immediately tells them Gay Men's Health Crisis, the original name of the organization now known publicly as GMHC. Their response to her provocative statement determines whether the date continues. Even today, being a straight woman in a community still dominated by gay men remains a challenge, she added.

There was a kind of loneliness in and around the activism that was occurring. That was a piece in and of itself that was very powerful. It's improved now because there's more diversity in the office, in the trenches. Donors are more diverse. It's still a struggle to meet men and have a relationship. And I flirt whenever I can. [9]

Fag Hags, Divas and Moms

The Medical Establishment
and Their Patients

I was quite visibly pregnant, and I was walking into the [intensive care unit to visit an AIDS patient] when one of the residents, a male resident, said, "Are you really sure you want to go in that room?" And I said, "What do you mean?" I had to stop and think before I understood what he was saying, and then I said, "Of course I do." But that marks when I first began to think, Gee, could we get this? It had not occurred to me before that this was something that doctors could get. - Dr. Molly Cooke, San Francisco General Hospital [1]

In the beginning, no one understood what they were seeing.

So, when critically ill young men showed up in doctor offices and emergency rooms, displaying symptoms rarely seen by medical professionals, no one was quite sure what to do.

In 1983, the CDC issued strict guidelines for making - or rather, avoiding - contact with patients known to be infected with bloodborne pathogens, especially AIDS. These protocols seemed horrific then, but still feel horrific now. Anyone coming in contact with a patient donned protective gowns and gloves. They wore masks and goggles. Patients were isolated in rooms with signs posted on the door, warning anyone who entered. Meals were served with disposable dishes and utensils, but too often the trays were left in hallways by food service personnel too frightened to enter the room. After usage, bed linens and clothing were burned. Such draconian measures were not applied to patients with more infectious diseases like Hepatitis B.

The resulting stigma condemned those with AIDS to negligent treatment, harassment and discrimination. Four years later, another CDC report recommended what they now called universal precautions. It was to be assumed that all patients - not just those obviously with AIDS - could be carrying infectious viruses in their blood. Wearing gloves for the medical community became mandatory for contact with all patients. Today we think nothing of it.

The possibility of infection was always there for the people who treated patients with AIDS. In a culture where being covered with blood had previously been considered a badge of honor, now every encounter could prove potentially fatal.

Dr. Constance Wofsy, who co-founded the AIDS program with Dr. Paul Volberding at San Francisco General Hospital in 1983, preferred to ignore the dangers - even when she rose to associate chief of infectious diseases.

[No, I wasn't afraid.] I was too gripped...We were people with a cause, and like any cause you become overzealous, I think. The people early on who worked on the AIDS ward almost flouted safety precautions. Our original infection control measures were written as "You do not need to wear gloves to examine the patient except for..." We became patient advocates to the exclusion of our own anxieties or rational observation of the data that was in front of us. [2]

They worked in a profession where the majority regarded the care of people with AIDS as optional. Given a choice at that time, almost 50% of primary care physicians would refuse to treat them. Only one quarter of them believed office-based professionals should be required to treat people with AIDS.

When Dr. Carol Brosgart became director of the Alta Bates community hospital AIDS program in Berkeley, CA in 1987, she found that the program did not have unanimous workplace support. Some of the medical staff believed AIDS was not their problem, that those patients should be shipped across the bridge to San Francisco with the other dying gay men. She could not escape the prejudice, even as a new employee.

> I was sort of a pariah because the disease I cared for was basically a pariah. I remember within a few days of coming, being in the elevator, and someone said, "Hi, are you a new doctor?" "Yes, I am, my name's Carol Brosgart. I run the new AIDS program." And just as we were about to shake hands...he took his hand away from me. And then he said, "Oh, I'm sorry; I guess you can't get AIDS that way." ...Well, it was incredibly distasteful to be treated as if you were a leper, just because you cared for people others saw as lepers. [3]

Sometimes fear got the better of good people.

Kathleen Pooler, undated
(photo courtesy of
Kathleen Pooler)

Kathleen Pooler was Nursing Administrative Director of the emergency room at Crouse-Irving Hospital in Syracuse in 1982.

> I witnessed first-hand the havoc it wreaked on its victims as we cared for emaciated, gravely-ill patients with multiple skin sores and a new kind of pneumonia, recently identified as Pneumocystis Carinii Pneumonia. I also witnessed the fear among the staff. It all unfolded in slow, agonizing motion as we

tried to move forward to provide the best care we could for our patients while protecting ourselves. *(4)*

Two years later, Pooler's cousin Bob, who managed traveling Broadway shows, died. No one in the family ever spoke of him being gay, much less that he died from AIDS. But that was early on, when newspapers reported that a death came after "a long illness". So, Bob's mother insisted that he died from cancer.

Straight women who worked as doctors, nurses and other professionals also had to confront the possibility of infection as it related to their families. Dr. Molly Cooke of San Francisco General Hospital practiced with her husband, pioneering AIDS expert Dr. Paul Volberding. And while they both responded to the dangers of treating their patients in very different ways, there was one issue that affected them both equally.

> "At the end of '82 we had several discussions about if we were going to have another baby because - and it sounds so melodramatic now - but it was not clear how safe what we were doing was. And I didn't want to go ahead and have another baby and then discover that one or both of us was not going to live to see the baby grow up. So, there was a very real sense of danger, that the work was potentially dangerous, and you just didn't know exactly how dangerous it was." *(5)*

Straight women physicians in the AIDS community faced complicated work/home balance issues. The damned if you do, damned if you don't feeling and its attendant guilt played out in ways all women will recognize. Marriages suffer, whether or not their husbands are in the same field. But with their patients' fragile health to consider, it's not surprising that Dr. Brosgart declared to Dr. Wofsy that working with AIDS patients is not just a full-time job, but a "full-time life."

> I remember talking to Connie when I went to [the International AIDS Meeting in Stockholm in 1988]. It meant missing my oldest daughter's high school graduation and other daughter's eighth birthday. And it was a big decision. And my kids said it

was okay, and I did it, and I loved the Stockholm meeting, but I felt very bad. And the year - I guess '91 - which was the Italian meeting, and Connie and I had a number of things planned in and around that meeting, at the last minute I called Connie and said, "Connie I'm not going to go. I've just been gone too much." It was a day or two before I was supposed to go and [my daughter] burst into tears. She wanted her mommy to be there. And I canceled...I think you just try to do your best, and sometimes it isn't your best and everyone's going to be a little disappointed. [6]

Medical professionals working with AIDS patients found themselves treating demographic groups that were not their usual patients. These included injection drug use and the chronically homeless, both who already lacked regular health care. Caring for them demanded a steep learning curve and team approach. In addition, those who assumed all their patients were heterosexual had to contend with a whole new world of homosexual men and a frank discussion of their sexual practices. Dr. Cooke found that she and other women were more comfortable with the subject than their straight male colleagues. And her curiosity was piqued by making an important connection.

Dr. Molly Cooke and
Dr. Paul Volberding, undated (ucsf.edu)

There was such a strong reaction to the number of sexual partners. People were just floored...seeing people's health problems so linked to their sexual histories was startling. It was like there was sex everywhere. And we were frankly fascinated by what did people do at the technical level that enabled them to have so many partners. Heterosexual sex is just not that quick. [7]

The medical system did not make things easy for those with HIV/AIDS, especially women, for whom an accurate diagnosis was rare in those early days. The greatest influx of the sickest patients could be found in public hospitals. By the mid-1980s, 5% of public hospitals - most located in San Francisco, Los Angeles and New York City - were treating 50% of the country's AIDS patients.

These patients had little or no insurance, no access to regular care or even a dependable support system. They filled the clinics to overflowing, and for women, the waits for care were even longer. That's because until January,1992, as far as the federal government and medical community were concerned, women were not at risk for HIV. Women's concerns were dismissed. They were actively discouraged from being tested, because a negative diagnosis was presumed.

There was an urgent activist slogan that arose during this era, showcasing the illogical belief: "Women don't get AIDS. They just die from it." The slogan was all too accurate, as Mary Jordan, a 24-year old woman in Chicago, found:

In 1986, an ex-boyfriend called me to advise me that he was HIV-positive. I took the test in April 1987, against the advice of AIDS hotline volunteers and my physician. When I called these hotlines or spoke with my doctor, they asked, "Are you an IV drug user or were you ever?" and "Are you promiscuous?" Since I was not either, their advice was not to take the test. Since my last sexual encounter was with that boyfriend in 1982, I was told not to worry because "HIV was not being spread in Chicago during the years 1979-1982."

I chose to disregard their advice and set my mind to rest by taking the test. The diagnosis was HIV-positive. [8]

Jordan's experience was not unusual, but she, like others in the community took charge of herself and her health. She looked for a support group that would address her fears and needs. There were many such groups for gay men, both in Chicago and other cities. But there were none for straight women like herself. Desperate, she joined the IV drug user group. There she met another woman who had been infected the same way she had. Within three years, the core membership of the group was dead.

One of the challenges of working in medicine is understanding and maintaining boundaries with patients. The trust patients place in their medical team - doctors, nurses, clinicians, social workers - is not given lightly. A relationship of trust must be established and maintained, but always within in the boundaries of professionalism. One of the criticism of women doctors was that they would be unable to control their emotions to maintain that distance. They had to be conscious of the perception that they were too close to their patients to treat them effectively and objectively.

People with HIV/AIDS were the first visible group to demand a different kind of relationship. They were a new breed of patient, and the first activists of the epidemic. They were not passive recipients of medical care. They demanded to be partners with their medical team, insisted that their questions be answered and their wishes respected. This new paradigm was outlined in The Denver Principles, a document created at the Denver PWA Conference in 1983 by six gay HIV-positive men. It has served as a blueprint not just for people with AIDS but for anyone with serious health challenges:

We condemn attempts to label us as 'victims,' a term that implies defeat, and we are only occasionally 'patients,' a term that implies passivity, helplessness, and dependence upon the care of others. We are 'People With AIDS.'.

Recommendations for all people:

1. *Support us in our struggle against those who would fire us from our jobs, evict us from our homes, refuse to touch us or separate us from our loved ones, our community or our peers, since available evidence does not support the view that AIDS can be spread by casual, social contact.*

2. *Don't scapegoat people with AIDS and blame us for the epidemic or generalize about our lifestyles.*

Recommendations for people with AIDS:

1. *Form caucuses to choose their own representatives, to deal with the media, to choose their own agenda and to plan their own strategies.*

2. *Be involved at every level of decision-making and specifically serve on the boards of directors of provider organizations.*

3. *Be included in all AIDS forums with equal credibility as other participants, to share their own experiences and knowledge.*

4. *Substitute high-risk sexual behaviors with lower-risk ones for People With AIDS who would risk endangering their current partners; we feel people with AIDS have an ethical responsibility to inform their potential sexual partners of their health status.*

Rights of People With AIDS.

1. *To as full and satisfying sexual and emotional lives as anyone else.*

2. *To quality medical treatment and quality social service provision without discrimination of any form including sexual orientation, gender, diagnosis, economic status or race.*

3. *To full explanations of all medical procedures and risks, to choose or refuse their treatment modalities, to refuse to participate in research without jeopardizing their treatment and to make informed decisions about their*

lives.

4. *To privacy, to confidentiality of medical records, to human respect and to choose who their significant others are.*

5. *To live and die with dignity. (9)*

Reading this from a 21st century vantage point one must wonder how these demands could be considered controversial. In 1983, however, this proud visibility and determination by people with AIDS was new. The medical community had no previous experience with pro-active patients who were creating a new dynamic of care.

Rather than acquiescing to the medical professional's knowledge and experience, people with HIV/AIDS educated themselves and emerged as experts of equal standing. Even veteran AIDS expert Dr. Anthony Fauci admitted of AIDS patients, "They educated us." The concept was radical and met initially with great resistance by the medical community.

For many medical professionals, the ability to maintain that emotional distance - and the power dynamic of doctor over patient - was challenged when working in the AIDS community. For some clinicians, witnessing the cruel treatment of those in their care inspired the medical people to become fierce advocates for their patients. Many AIDS doctors found themselves fighting their own bosses.

But for many doctors, at a time when they knew that virtually all of their patients would die, the concept of a "good death" changed. A common definition would be that a person dies at home, pain-free, surrounded by loved ones. These AIDS patients, though, were often homeless or indigent, living with friends or in one of the few AIDS-related housing programs that began to spring up in the mid-1980s. The doctors couldn't reach out to family, because many patients had been abandoned by their families and refused any attempt at reconciliation. Their normal expectations were challenged. But, as Dr. Brosgart describes, they found a path to something everyone would agree is a good definition of "good death".

What I want, I think, for all of my patients is to not die alone, to die comfortably without pain, and surrounded by people they love or things they love. [10]

Dr. Cooke believed that the key to the doctor-patient relationship was the willingness of the doctor to listen. Confronted by patients whose suffering led them to consider suicide, she did not feel comfortable aiding them in that goal. She would treat their depression if possible and manage their symptoms. These were conversations that most in the medical community were not skilled at having.

All of these women were trained to be dispassionate, to rely on their training to help their patients. But in a situation where the traditional boundaries were crossed every day, they also struggled about attending funerals and memorial services. The guilt and frustration associated with being unable to save their patients - along with the need for women doctors to prove their professionalism - may have influenced their decision. Some refused to go to any services, believing that honoring the memory of their patient crossed a final line, and perhaps being unwilling to face their patient's family and friends.

Many AIDS programs - in hospices, housing programs, clinics and hospitals - regularly held memorial services for patients who died. Those were different than traditional funerals. Unbound by religious orthodoxy or ethnic traditions, they focused on sharing stories and celebrating a life lost too soon.

Celebrating is exactly what Dr. Constance Wofsy did when she attended an event in 1995, just a year before she herself died from breast cancer. At the time, Wofsy was co-director of the University of California AIDS program at San Francisco General Hospital. Her enormous contributions included educating health care providers and co-founding AWARE (Association for Women's AIDS Research and Education). That nonprofit served high-risk women in the San Francisco Bay area and published some of the first research on that demographic.

Ten years earlier, a middle-school principal had invited Wofsy to speak to the students and parents about AIDS, to dispel anxieties while addressing stigma and prejudice, because one of the teachers had been diagnosed with the virus. Her rational, non-shaming information quieted the fears of adults and children alike.

She was back for the dedication of a new auditorium to be named for that teacher, now near death, who arrived on a stretcher with multiple oxygen tanks. It was really an opportunity for those present to express their love and appreciation. In addition to speeches and performances from the students, something happened that affected Wofsy very deeply. She was in awe as every single person walked up to that stretcher and hugged the dying teacher. AIDS, a cause for deep concern ten years earlier, was irrelevant. Dr. Wofsy had been transformed: the fear and anxiety she had been carrying around the epidemic for a decade was suddenly gone, replaced by a new and indomitable sense of determination.

Fag Hags, Divas and Moms

The Researchers

"A woman in science, they never do anything.
They are only good at caring for the home and babies.
Forget this dream." [1]

Francoise Barré-Sinoussi was finishing her PhD in retroviruses at the University of Paris when she met with a senior staff member at the Pasteur Institute, where she hoped to work. This advice he gave her – documented in the insensitive words above - was not unusual in 1975. Women were actively discouraged from pursuing careers in this male-dominated field. They were paid less than men and denied both tenure and advancement. They toiled in near-obscurity, their achievements often co-opted by the men they worked for, or even their subordinates. Some of their accomplishments, like those of the women depicted in the recent films *Hidden Figures* and *Rocket Girls*, are only recently coming to light, decades after the fact, and being commemorated.

Luckily, she did not take his advice.

While many straight women became involved in the AIDS community because of a personal connection, others were drawn by the professional challenge of the new, mysterious virus and its effects.

The early days of the epidemic were marked by an international battle over the right to claim discovery of the virus that caused AIDS. Dr. Robert Gallo at the National Institutes of Health in

Washington and Dr. Luc Montagnier at the Pasteur Institute in Paris waged a very public fight. It was a matter of American vs French science, with millions of dollars at stake for the patent on the first HIV tests, and the perceived appearance of greed on both sides.

Francoise Barré-Sinoussi worked with Montagnier at the Pasteur Institute in the early 1980's on retroviruses, a focus of her PhD studies. An infectious disease specialist invited them in 1982 to begin looking for the active agent in what would eventually be called AIDS. They were given a lymph node sample from a French patient to study for retrovirus activity.

Francoise Barré-Sinoussi,
Nobel Prize press conference, Stockholm,
Dec. 6, 2008

Their work to discover that activity was described by Barré-Sinoussi as "no problem at all." The process was deceptively simple, although the revelation would rock the medical world. When their initial findings naming the virus LAV (lymphadenopathy-associated virus) were published in Science in May, 1983, she was sure they had unraveled the medical mystery.

But what I didn't realize was the impact of the virus. I remember that I told my husband, who wasn't very happy because I wasn't very often at home, 'Don't worry, it's just you know, for one, two years maybe and then it will be over.' [2]

Bu it was only the beginning of what would become Barré-Sinoussi's life's work.

Scientists, medical practitioners, and therapists are cautioned to be objective in their work. Emotional attachments to patients are not only discouraged but prohibited. The AIDS epidemic, though, erased those lines. The landmark 1983 Denver Principles saw people with AIDS demanding an equal role in their care. Researchers who typically at a distance from patients, were not excused from this new dynamic.

The change was evident. Government bureaucrats in Washington were soon on a first-name basis with ACT UP members. Doctors and therapists were attending their patients' funerals. The relationship between men and women of science and people living and dying from AIDS was growing stronger, more intimate. For Barré-Sinoussi, the line between medical objectivity and personal emotionality was crossed in 1984.

The young virologist was invited to speak to staff at about her work. SF General was ground zero for HIV cases in the 1980s. The work being done in Paris was well-known by the hospital staff, as well as patients. Word spread that this famous French scientist was in the building. A doctor approached Barré-Sinoussi and explained that an AIDS patient, dying, had asked to see her. Thirty years later, the researcher recalled that day as a turning point in her career.

He had difficulty speaking, but I could see on his lips that he said, 'Thank you'...I was so totally, I didn't know what to say, and the doctor saw me and said, 'Ask him why.' And I did. I asked him why he thanked me and he said, 'Not for me, for the others.'

...Since that day I have that (image) in my mind...He took my hand and I still feel his hand in my hand today. [3]

Her commitment, both professional and personal, lasted

through decades of time-consuming work. It survived the stain of the international slug-fest between the Pasteur Institute and Robert Gallo at the National Institutes of Health, both battling over who deserved credit for discovering the virus. Being a researcher, poring over petri dishes in laboratories, did not protect Barré-Sinoussi from the emotional toll that the first fifteen years of the epidemic took on her. Where others rejoiced in 1996 at the dramatic results from the so-called cocktail of antiretroviral drugs, Barré-Sinoussi was surprised to have an opposite reaction.

"'I rapidly developed depression', she says flatly.

'Why?'

'Probably because so much stress accumulated on our (scientists) shoulders for years - to have seen people dying and feeling that we were not going fast enough, and when suddenly the data appeared of the combination treatment, that people were living, they were safe...and the fact that we were relieved - we just fell down.'"

For more than a year she stopped going to HIV events and conferences.

"When I reappeared among the community some of my colleagues said, "Oh, Francoise, it's a long time since we've seen you, what happened?' And I explained and they said, 'You too? Welcome to the club.' Despite not being alone in her reaction to the breakthrough, the manifestation of mental illness was alarming and bewildering." (4)

For the first time, she sought help, though anonymously. A year of antidepressants helped bring her back.

By 2008, when she shared the Nobel Prize in Physiology with Montagnier, Barré-Sinoussi's life had changed. Her husband, whom she had reluctantly neglected for years while staying late nights at the lab, immersed in research, had died. She doesn't speak to Montagnier, who she stopped working with in the late 1980s. Curiously, she has a better relationship with Gallo, contrary to media reports.

Her focus since then has largely centered on mother-to-child transmission of HIV and work in countries like Cameroon and Cambodia, where more than 90% of those with HIV are undergoing treatment. Like others in the field, she laments the lack of accurate and available sex education especially for young people. Policies affecting those groups, including HIV-criminalization and drug addiction criminalization, deepen the stigma that prevents those most in need from receiving information and treatment. She is equally frustrated by a growing complacency that leads to surges in infections among key demographic groups.

Though officially retired, Barré-Sinoussi continues to work. When asked if she thought she'd live to see a functional cure for HIV, she joked that it depended on how long she lived.

At the time Barré-Sinoussi was starting her career in Paris in 1975, Dr. Mathilde Krim was already an interferon researcher at Sloan-Kettering Medical Center in New York. She was married to Arthur Krim, an entertainment lawyer and head of United Artists movie studio. The high-profile couple was politically active in the civil rights movement as well as national Democratic politics. Her initial scientific curiosity about AIDS was further strengthened by the injustice connected to it: the homophobia and moralism directed at young gay men who were infected and dying.

Morality was important to Krim. Born in Italy to a Swiss father and Czech/German mother, she and her family moved to Geneva to escape the threat of World War II. When she was 18, Krim watched a newsreel of the liberation of concentration camps and was horrified by the skeletal survivors, as well as the mountains of corpses. Human rights had been a prominent topic of interest in her family.

But when the teenager went home and told her parents what she'd seen, they insisted it was not real. Krim pointed to that newsreel as the catalyst for her life's work: to ensure that humanity would never treat a group of people like that again. Her passion for justice was so strong, in fact, that she was involved in the Israeli underground, the Irgun, before she married Arthur Krim, a Jew, and converted.

Krim believed that her Sloan-Kettering interferon work could be critical to identifying the virus and developing treatment and eventually a cure. But when she approached private foundations for support in expanding her research to HIV, the response surprised her.

> The prevalent attitude, she later explained, was that the disease 'resulted from a sleazy lifestyle, drugs or kinky sex, and that certain people had learned their lesson and it served them right. That was the attitude, even on the part of respectable foundations that are supposed to be concerned about human welfare.' (5)

Krim had no patience with that kind of attitude. Science was science, she believed, with no room for discrimination or disapproval. In 1983, joined by fellow AIDS researcher Dr. Joseph Sonnabend and AIDS activist Michael Callen, she co-founded The AIDS Medical Foundation. The group was funded with $100,000 of her own money. In late 1985, AMF merged with the California-based National AIDS Research Foundation, started by Elizabeth Taylor to become the American Foundation for AIDS Research (amfAR). To more accurately reflect the organization's international reach, in 2005, amfAR became The Foundation for AIDS Research.

The doctor and the movie star were an unlikely pair. Though both wealthy and connected to powerful people, their focus and personalities were very different. Taylor was "front of the house". As the public (and glamorous) face of amfAR, she was ready and willing to testify on Capitol Hill, give interviews or headline fundraising events. Krim was a no-nonsense researcher, uncomfortable with the glitz required for fundraising and more doggedly focused on less flashy but crucial medical objectives.

Initially criticized for expanding amfAR's work beyond the US, Krim emphasized what researchers realized early on: that HIV is not bound by gender, race, ethnicity or nationality. When she focused on targeting heterosexual transmission, Sonnabend protested by leaving the organization. It's hard to believe now that the insistence on the urgency of halting heterosexual HIV transmission, particularly outside of the US, could be controversial. But Sonnabend and others reasonably worried that this new emphasis would justify the further marginalization of homosexuals during the epidemic.

At the same time, under rising criticism of her work with amfAR, Krim left Sloan-Kettering and her interferon research to fully concentrate on AIDS. That move was seen by some colleagues in the biomedical research community as proof of her lack of commitment to "real" research.

Like Taylor, Krim had no patience for the red tape typically associated with research grants. It was not unusual for a year or more to pass between application and award. So, amfAR began awarding grants, modest at first, within a few months of requests being submitted. When the science was moving quickly, the ability to grant funding for research in such a short amount of time was crucial to progress.

Her impatience was also directed at drug companies for outrageous pricing. (When AZT was introduced in 1987 by Burroughs Wellcome, a year's supply cost $10,000.) Krim also very publicly criticized the limitations of clinical trials, especially.

The protocol required a control group in a double-blind clinical trial. The control group received placebos. Neither the patient nor the people running the trial knew who was getting what. Her argument was that patients seeking experimental treatment for a fatal disease should not be given placebos. That false hope was not only cruel, but deadly. Equally egregious was that clinical trials systematically shut out women and people of color - two growing demographics in the epidemic. These inequities would also become a target of early ACT UP demonstrations in the summer of

1987, the activist group's first year of existence. They held a week-long protest of clinical trial policies at Memorial Sloan-Kettering, Krim's former workplace.

For her tireless work, Dr. Mathilde Krim was given the Presidential Medal of Freedom in 1990, bestowed on her by President Bill Clinton. In his address, Clinton acknowledged the researcher's commitment to medicine as well as her compassion for patients.

By the mid-1990s, the HAART drugs became available and many with AIDS were brought back from the brink of death to reasonably good health. But the community-wide exhaustion created by the fifteen-year epidemic was beginning to show. Many ACT UP chapters had imploded. "AIDS fatigue" had already begun settling in among fundraisers and advocates. The initial urgency was gone, but the epidemic was not. Like many organizations, amfAR suffered financially as people presumed the epidemic was over and no longer required robust funding. But Krim - who had taken a leave during her husband's final illness and death in 1994 - returned with renewed determination.

Dr. Mathilde Krim and
Mr. Leather,
1995 NYC Pride Parade
(photographer unknown)

You know, I'm an old lady now. Sometimes I look out on my garden and think, maybe I should stop and spend some time on the flowers. But I look and see the destruction AIDS has caused, the young, vital people it has killed, and I know I cannot stop. [6]

Dr. Krim was another prominent medical person who had no time for the traditional distance established between patient and practitioner. She testified for funding on Capitol Hill and then worked closely with people with HIV/AIDS right through her mid-80s. Hundreds of thousands considered her an ally, an inspiration and a friend.

Her willingness to be immersed on a personal level led Dr. Krim to surprising places, as Candida Scott Piel, who served as amfAR's liaison to the LGBT community from 1994-2002 explains:

I did various fundraisers for amfAR, including the Mr. Leather contest. In 1995, the winner was Andy Borden, a tall, handsome, lovely guy. Arthur Krim had recently died, and Dr. Krim was pretty low. I thought, 'She should come meet Mr. Leather! This might be fun!' I introduced them, and it was like the rest of us just disappeared. They fell madly in love with each other and it was the sweetest thing in the world. They had coffee, and the photographer Morgan Gwenwald got a photo in which Dr. Krim climbed a library ladder to be in a shot with Mr. Leather, because he was like six-foot-seven. They adored each other. When amfAR was participating in the 1995 Pride Parade, we thought it wouldn't be dignified for Dr. Krim to be on a float, but maybe she could ride in a Jeep? The prospect of riding down Fifth Avenue in the back of a Jeep with Mr. Leather, and she was all in. It was a match made in heaven and a delightful fluke." [7]

When Dr. Krim died on January 15, 2018 at the age of 91, accolades poured in from leaders in the global AIDS community and individuals who testified that her tireless work had saved their lives. Memories were shared online of her ability to bridge factions that were often at odds - activists, scientists, celebrities. Her legacy was unique and unmatched. She was respected not only for the research that drove her to understand this virus, but for aligning with those who were on the margins of society. Peter Staley, an early leader in ACT UP and former board member of amfAR, is clear on her legacy.

> If Larry Kramer was the father of AIDS activism, Mathilde was the mother. For the survivors of the plague years, there was no one we loved more. She fought for us from day one, using her scientific reputation to beat back the stigma we faced. Mathilde was one of the first scientists and socialites to defend ACT UP, and she deeply embraced TAG's work. She was my mentor, and a constant source of inspiration in the fight to end AIDS. [8]

In the long and complicated history of AIDS, there is one woman who qualifies as a pioneering researcher, though she never conducted research on her own. In fact, she died of cervical cancer thirty years before the first article appeared in the *New York Times* in July of 1981, warning in Times newspeak of a new cancer, affecting homosexual men.

Few people knew the name of this woman until 2010, when Rebecca Skloot's best-selling *The Immortal Life of Henrietta Lacks* was published. The story of an African-American woman whose cancer cells were harvested without the permission of herself or her family, only to then be used for decades by others who profited off of their medical uniqueness, engaged and enraged many. The research conducted over the years on those cells has led to groundbreaking discoveries: the development of the HPV vaccine to prevent cervical cancer, Jonas Salk's ability to test the polio vaccine on human cells, and the mapping of the Human Genome Project.

Her cells have shown particular promise in virology, allowing scientists to create battle plans against herpes, Zika, measles, mumps and HIV.

They discovered, for instance, that the type of white blood cell called a T-cell sports a surface protein called CD4, which is what HIV uses to enter the cell. When CD4 was added to HeLa cells, they could be infected with HIV, allowing HIV drugs to be tested on HeLa cells. [9]

Sha Jin, associate professor in nanogenetics at the University of Arkansas, Fayetteville, unveiled research findings in 2010, again using HeLa cells, that had wide-ranging implications for drug testing. Not only were HeLa cells instrumental in identifying an enzyme produced when healthy cells are infected with HIV, but they helped determine the toxicity of various drugs used to treat the virus.

It's odd to think that a disenfranchised, exploited and ultimately forgotten African-American woman who died in 1951 deserves a place in this book. But her unwitting and groundbreaking contributions to HIV/AIDS research are indisputable. So, her story lives on. Against her will and against her permission, to be sure, she continues to help save lives.

Fag Hags, Divas and Moms

The Spiritual Community

"AIDS is our teacher. This disease holds deep lessons for everyone
in this room, and it will have lessons to teach the world."
Matthew Fox, progressive Catholic theologian [1]

The relationship between the AIDS community and religious institutions has been fraught from the beginning.

In 1979, Rev. Jerry Falwell co-founded The Moral Majority, the first of many LGBT hate groups that espouse so-called traditional values: pro-life, pro-family, pro-American, pro-morality. The Moral Majority declared war against anyone they perceived as being at odds with those values. Falwell had positioned himself as anti-gay, aligning himself with Anita Bryant's 1977 anti-gay "Save Our Children" campaign. They had successfully overturned a Dade County, Florida, ordinance that prohibited discrimination based on sexual orientation.

Under Falwell's leadership, The Moral Majority quickly became a major lobbying force; they were credited with delivering the white evangelical vote for Ronald Reagan in 1980. That power no doubt fueled the brazen refusal of the Reagan administration to address the epidemic until tens of thousands had already died. As far as Falwell was concerned, the gay community and AIDS were synonymous. And they got what they deserved. Reagan, naturally, was reluctant to upset his voter base by supporting AIDS research. So, he placated Bible-thumpers and the death toll mounted.

The Moral Majority's disgust with what they labeled the "homosexual lifestyle" had no limits. Years later, even as America grew more supportive of LGBT rights, Falwell was still railing. He went as far as to attribute the September 11th attacks to God's anger against homosexuals.

In the 1990s, the world-famous Rev. Billy Graham first stated that he believed AIDS was God's way of judging homosexuals, an assertion he later retracted.

Things weren't any better in the Catholic Church. In 2005, Shortly after his election to the papacy, Pope Benedict XVI told senior African clergy that AIDS could not be cured with condoms. As late as 2010, there was still a Vatican-sourced debate on the moral implications of condom use. That same year, after years of vocal opposition from church leaders on the continent, the Pope relented a bit: as long as condoms were not used for family planning and were not considered a 'real or moral' solution to the AIDS epidemic, they could be considered a first step towards accepting responsibility for not sharing disease. But the damage had already been done by his 2009 assertion that condoms actually spread HIV. This message contributed to the deaths of millions, including in notably in heavily Catholic countries in Africa, where the church taught that condoms were strictly forbidden.

Women in African Muslim countries faced similar barriers to information and services. Positive Muslims, an awareness-raising and support group primarily focusing on straight women and HIV/AIDS, was founded in South Africa in 2000. Rather than following a strict Islamic interpretation of disease as a test from Allah, they developed what they call a "theology of compassion." focusing on Allah as a compassionate being. Their research convinced them that women are the most vulnerable group in the Muslim community because of patriarchal religious and cultural traditions.

The organization was co-founded by Farid Esack, a prominent Islamic scholar and Faghmeda Miller, the first HIV-positive woman in South Africa to go public with her diagnosis. That visibility was not welcomed: women are supposed to remain silent. Some members of the Muslim Judicial Council and other organizations within the Muslim community believed that AIDS is a curse, and because of that, she should have been stoned to death. But that criticism did not deter her. She continues to carry on.

In the early days, Catholic clergy refused sacraments to those with AIDS, both anointing of the sick (a sacrament for those who are gravely ill) and funeral masses. There were loopholes, however: if the mode of transmission was anything other than gay sex, prostitution or drug use - thus deeming the dead Catholic an innocent victim - exceptions to these bans could be made. Occasionally, a priest would agree to bestow the sacraments, as long as the dying repented for his sinful ways.

It is known as "Stop the Church!" The ACT UP demonstration at St. Patrick's Cathedral in New York City on Dec. 11, 1989, drawing 4,500 protestors, showcased the Church's moral crimes. Activists railed against Cardinal O'Connor for opposing condom use to prevent infection, and lobbying against HIV education in the school, as well as his promotion of institutional homophobia. Their protests were backed by medical facts, but their actions that morning were considered by many - even within ACT UP - as too extreme. An independent faction of ACT UP members protested inside the cathedral, screaming out slogans and lying in the aisles as an act of civil disobedience. One activist, a former altar boy living with AIDS named Tom Keane, crumpled the communion host in protest. Critics called the tactics disrespectful and the widespread condemnation across the globe overshadowed ACT UP's message. This landmark action did nothing to improve relations between the Church and the AIDS community.

When the Alexian Brothers, a religious order, opened a residential program for people with AIDS in Chicago in 1989, reactions ranged from skepticism to hostility. There were few AIDS ministries in those days and even fewer housing programs. People who'd been ostracized and condemned as sinners by their own faith communities were not necessarily eager to live in a place where the executive director was a priest and they were greeted everyday by a crucifix on the wall.

In the African-American community, life revolves around the church. But deep-seated homophobia impeded progress on HIV education and treatment among this hard-hit demographic for many years. Needle exchange programs, proven to slow down infection rates among IV-drug users, were seen as encouraging illegal drug use in communities of color already ravaged by addiction.

But to ultimately make advancements in fighting HIV in these communities, peace had to be made with churches. And not just in the US. In sub-Saharan Africa, where over 7,000,000 people are HIV-positive, INERELA+, an interfaith network of religious leaders, is fighting Pentecostal churches that purportedly offer miracle blessings and a cure for AIDS. These self-described healers conduct a public ritual healing, burn the patient's anti-retroviral drugs and pronounce them cured – all for a price.

There were bright spots on the religious front, however: the AIDS National Interfaith Network declared without hesitation that AIDS was not God's punishment. Individual congregations of many faith traditions, defying their elders and hierarchy, have stepped up to provide support for people with HIV/AIDS.

In religious circles, there have always been women who stepped up to make a difference - an achievement all the more powerful where they lacked standing in the male-based faith communities. One of the most striking examples was a woman in Arkansas, who started a program common in big cities, but with one unique twist.

Newly divorced, her children in college, Trudy James moved from Kansas to Little Rock in 1989. There she began a hospital chaplaincy residency at the University of Arkansas Medical Center. Unsure of what she wanted to do with her life and barred from the priesthood in the Episcopal Church, she was hoping the experience could provide personal direction.

During that one-year program she worked with eight patients with AIDS: four men, four women, four black, four white, ranging in age from 16-54. Only two of them were visited by family; none by clergy or fellow church members. Medical staff refused to enter their rooms to assess them; neither did nursing staff provide care or even bring in meals. It was a scenario that was repeated every day in small towns and big cities around the world.

As her residency drew to a close, Trudy James' supervisor encouraged her to apply for an unusual job: Arkansas CareTeam Coordinator for Regional AIDS Interfaith Network (RAIN). She would be working to engage lay people from churches and synagogues to support people with AIDS. At first, Trudy believed that was an impossible goal. There was nothing to suggest that such a program had much chance of success anywhere, much less Arkansas. But then, a personal connection changed everything.

Trudy received a letter from her mother, relating the news that a friend had died from AIDS. Since he was the mayor's son, the cause of death was hidden to avoid political scandal. There would be no funeral or public acknowledgement. It was as if the man never existed.

There was nothing unique about such dishonesty resulting from shame; Trudy had seen it before. But now, the fact that it happened to someone she'd loved since childhood, compelled her to apply for the AIDS program coordinator position. She was hired The responses to her appointment varied:

> My friends told me I was either quite brave - or truly crazy. My mother was sure I would catch AIDS and maybe even go to hell for associating with homosexuals. My children applauded. (2)

Trudy's program was directed at recruiting and educating volunteers from faith communities that were committed to pastoral care. They represented a broad spectrum of denominations: Catholic, Methodist, Episcopalian and Presbyterian churches, as well as Disciples of Christ, Unitarian Universalist, Metropolitan Community Church (MCC), African Methodist Episcopal (AME) and synagogues. Teams could not require patient attendance or adherence to any faith system. They were expected to "be with" their Care Partner rather than "do for" them: again, a partnership model that was a sea change from previous volunteer efforts.

Even Trudy approached this program with initial skepticism. Could these teams from faith communities earn the trust of people whose illness made them outcasts to society - a status exacerbated by religious dogma? Could these teams overcome any initial

Unnamed Arkansas CareTeam member
with her CarePartners
(photo courtesy of Trudy James)

personal fears or negative beliefs? Could they find enough common ground to work together, to ask for and receive support, to offer unconditional love? And could buddy teams resist the temptation to evangelize?

In that era, most people looked at HIV/AIDS as an urban problem, something that only affects people who live in big cities. The fallacy persists. When Trudy's program began, over half of the people with AIDS in Arkansas lived outside of cities. By 1997, the "Love Makes a Difference in AIDS" slogan was not only visible but represented 127 CareTeams (1,500 volunteers) in forty Arkansas cities, towns and villages.

While their focus was primarily on the person with AIDS, the CareTeam also addressed the needs of family members who could be angry, scared, or hostile towards the CarePartner. Team members were directed to not coerce family members to behave a certain way, but to allow their personal feelings to be expressed. In fact, many families were completely absent. Those who chose to be involved often preferred to believe that their loved one had cancer or another respectable disease. Anything was preferable to AIDS.

The one thing that was expressly forbidden of CareTeam members was proselytizing. Occasionally, a partner or a family member would ask to come to church services. Those requests were thoughtfully discussed because CareTeams could not function effectively if there was even a hint of pressure. They wanted partners to know that people of faith would support them because their work was a natural outgrowth of that faith and was not dependent on the partner's participation. And while some CarePartners wanted to reconnect with their spirituality, none were required.

The power of James' program for people with AIDS was not so much the practical support, but the emotional support. And that connection went both ways, as one of her Arkansas team members admitted shortly after the death of her CarePartner in 1993:

> I never knew I could love someone like my own child...yet, that is the way I loved him. He inspired me, he enriched my life, he brought me joy. I learned from him. I spoiled him because I wanted to - he needed to experience that. He had never known the joy of family life - I hope we gave him a taste of it... [3]

Trudy's program was a success. But what felt like continuous grieving eventually took an emotional toll. In addition, the increasing demands of fundraising and administration left her feeling cut off from her true calling. She decided it was time for a change. Trudy moved to Seattle to be closer to two of her children and her newborn grandson. After a year-long sabbatical, she replicated her program there, training 70 teams in the Puget Sounds over the next ten years. The CareTeams also welcomed interfaith teams as well as two specifically African-American teams to focus on destigmatizing the virus in the African Methodist Episcopal Church community. In 2000 they merged with Seattle Shanti, an established one-on-one emotional support program, to create Multifaith Works, whose dedication continues today.

By 1991, there were 2,810 AIDS ministries throughout the US, which sounds like a lot until you consider that there were several hundred thousand faith communities in existence. Not all the AIDS ministries were affiliated with one particular church or congregation. Many stood alone, deliberately nondenominational in philosophy. Some were focused on a narrow range of services: meal delivery, housing, child services. But all were committed to direct service and the need to physically connect with their clients.

There was a duality in the Catholic Church during the early plague years: while the hierarchy banned the use of condoms and refused to bury those who died from AIDS, there was a different dynamic among the ranks. Nuns could be counted on to reach out with love and compassion.

For 200 years, the Sisters of Charity of New York, in the spirit of St. Elizabeth Seton, have ministered to the sick. Their hospital, St. Vincent's in Greenwich Village, became the epicenter of the AIDS epidemic. By 1985, Sr. Patrice Murphy, SC, supervised 90 AIDS patients in the hospice program.

Nearby was St. Veronica's Catholic Church, on Christopher Street. An anchor of the community since 1890, it was surrounded by the epidemic. Though the pastor himself had requested funding to open an AIDS hospice in the rectory, the Archdiocese co-opted the idea as their own and turned over the building to Mother Teresa's nuns in 1985. Terri Cook, a former parishioner involved in trying to save the church since it closed in 2017, told *America* magazine the building needed to be preserved as a testament to the parish, not to the hierarchy of the church.

In 1991, an AIDS memorial was established at St. Veronica's to commemorate the scores of men in their community who died. Likely due to parishioner opposition, the memorial was not immediately visible on entering the church. In the choir loft, at the top of rickety wooden steps, one would find rows of names on plaques, and a little table sparsely adorned with flowers and a candle. That same year an interfaith service was held for those dying as well as to remember the dead. It was an annual event until the church closed in 2017.

Sr. Betty Brucker, a Franciscan Sister of Mercy served as executive director and president of St. Mary's Health Center in St. Louis from 1975-1991. To lead a medical center in the early years of the epidemic meant facing not only this new, frightening virus, but the stigma attached to it. Patients being released from the hospital often had no home to return to, after being rejected by their families or evicted by landlords. Working with a variety of Christian denominations and a local rabbi, Sr. Betty started the Doorways Interfaith AIDS residence program.

At the same time in New Orleans, Sr. Marcy Romine volunteered with Project Lazarus, the Catholic archdiocesan agency for people with HIV/AIDS. Founded in 1985 on the top floor of an old convent to provide hospice services, it grew, continuing to serve people with HIV/AIDS with transitional housing: a place to live as well as to die. Sr. Marcy loved everything about it: New Orleans's culture and food, as well as working in the HIV community. But, like many, the work took a toll on her. In 2002 she moved to St. Louis to take the position of vocation minister for her order, the Franciscan Sister of Our Lady of Perpetual Help. But the pull to New Orleans was strong, and in 2011, she returned, this time to CrescentCare, the NO/AIDS Task Force community health center, to serve as Director of Special Projects until her death in 2017.

Not all nuns were beacons of hope. One in particular remains a controversial figure, even after her canonization by the Catholic Church in 2016.

Mother Teresa (now St. Teresa of Calcutta) founded the Missionary Sisters of Charity in 1950. She became a media celebrity, sought out by politicians and religious leaders eager to be seen in the company of a holy woman. Her donors included Charles Keating, the financier involved in the infamous savings and loan collapse, and Jean-Claude Duvalier, the excessively cruel dictator of Haiti from 1971 until his 1986 overthrow.

Many of the hundreds of missions she opened around the world were dedicated to AIDS patients. But they were not medical facilities as we recognize them. Her belief that there is beauty in suffering overshadowed the use of conservative pain relief. At the same time, she professed to fighting AIDS, Mother Teresa spoke out globally against the use of condoms.

Not all spiritual support was limited to mainstream religion, or organized religion at all. Many alternative spiritual organizations, arising during the New Age movement, offered support groups, personal empowerment and meditative arts. It's not surprising that many people who were condemned by their own religious traditions turned to these other sources of comfort. After all, these alternative healers offered effective emotional support, unburdened by the structure of any traditional or punitive religion. Of course, some offered dubious cures or treatment that did not deliver the miracles they promised.

Several women led these alternative spiritual organizations. Most prominent were Louise Hay, Marianne Williamson and Cynthia O'Neal. Their programs were lauded and helped tens of thousands address their illnesses, and even their deaths. But like Mother Teresa, they were also accused of profiting off the vulnerable and dying.

One of the early AIDS support groups in New York City was Friends in Deed, an organization that had its roots in Marianne Williamson's Manhattan Center for Living. Its founder, Cynthia O'Neal, did not come from a social service or medical background. She lived in the elegant Dakota on the Upper West Side of Manhattan with her husband of 35 years, actor Patrick O'Neal. Her neighbors in the building included Leonard Bernstein, John Lennon and Yoko Ono. Like many straight women in the community, O'Neal faced disapproval and suspicion from her friends and family for her involvement.

> Patrick had watched me become more and more involved with the AIDS community over the preceding years, and I imagine that he'd most likely been picturing me in the role of administrator/organizer. I suppose that watching me actually standing there at the head of a large packed room, facilitating a group of nearly a hundred people, dealing with life-and-death issues, put the whole thing in a new light. Perhaps he saw that I had acquired certain skills he didn't know I had.

> I suspect our friends shared some of Patrick's puzzlement. There are many good longtime friends who had known me

as someone who was most often focused on such important matters as finding the perfect Italian shoes, the perfect frame for the picture, the perfect black satin jacket, the perfect wine for the coq au vin, the best possible seats for opening night. What must any of them have thought when I cancelled our dinner date because instead, I was choosing to spend my evening in the emergency room with someone I barely knew? [4]

Friends in Deed proved to be a unique support for her as well after her husband died in September of 1994. In January,1996, she received a call from a young man, Jonathan Larson. She knew him slightly: he'd attended Big Groups at FiD with his best friend, Matthew O'Grady, who was a client. Big Groups functioned much like 12-step programs: group shares, privacy within the group, reliance on higher powers. O'Neal noticed that Larson listened intently to everything discussed, but assumed he was just being supportive. Larson eventually approached O'Neal with a request: He wanted her to speak to the cast of the musical he'd just written, because it dealt with issues around AIDS. His show was simply called *Rent*.

O'Neal had a whole list of reasons to beg off: there was a nasty ice storm going on, she'd never get a cab, it was all the way down in the East Village. She tried to gracefully decline when she heard a voice in the back of her head:

What are you thinking? Young actors doing a show about life and death and love and fear and AIDS? There's only one possible answer. The answer is yes. [5]

Rather than give a talk, she asked Larson to have questions prepared for her to answer, and she headed downtown. The afternoon with the cast energized her, though she had to leave before the rehearsal started. She promised to make the time to listen to the CD that Larson had mailed her.

Three days later, on January 25, 1996, O'Neal walked into her office to find a message waiting for her: Jonathan Larson had suddenly died the night before. He was only 35. (Only later would she learn that Larson had succumbed to an undiagnosed aortic aneurysm.) It was at Larson's memorial service on February 3rd at the Minetta Lane Theater that O'Neal finally heard the powerful score he'd created for the production. A few days after that, she and Matthew O'Grady attended a performance of *Rent*.

Cynthia and Anthony
Rapp, Rent screening,
Symphony Space, NYC,
Nov. 22, 2005
(Linda Lenzi @
BroadwayWorld.com)

Larson's intense interest in the Big Group discussions was not just for his best friend's benefit. The support group in the musical was clearly modeled after Friends in Deed. The show itself was about the searching for acceptance, the spiritual support and friendship that Friends in Deed was built upon.

Even before Friends in Deed came into existence, Marianne Williamson and Louise Hay were drawing crowds to their lectures in Los Angeles. Their philosophies were similar: let go of the anger and fear of AIDS and death. They believed in the mind-body connection - that a shift in attitude, from negative to positive thinking, would improve your health. Both Hay's and Williamson's books were best-sellers.

There is certainly some truth in the benefits of a positive attitude. Their support groups, initially begun in their homes as early as 1983, were attended by those who previously felt they had no hope. These groups offered alternatives to organized religion, providing less judgment and much more in the way of acceptance and support for those facing mortality But, there were naysayers of this new mindset. Many hated the implied New Age message from Hay that people were responsible for their own disease, because of bad attitudes. Others cited the high costs of these so-called evolved modalities. Hay's weekend-long workshops, which she took on the road, could cost several hundred dollars to attend.

Long-term survivor Sheri Lewis dismisses the criticisms of the New Age self-help prophets:

> And why wouldn't we have been angry then? For many of us, nobody was going to help. We were on our own. From Louise, I learned how to nurture myself as the mother I wanted to be - and would not be able to become because of HIV. My goal was not to cure myself, but to stay alive until effective treatment emerged. I would visualize myself being alive and well, one day telling my story as history - as I am doing right now. [6]

Fag Hags, Divas and Moms

The Moms

"Mothers want to fix it. Mothers want to make it better.
And it just drives you nuts when that doesn't work."
- Anne King to her son, Mark S. King [1]

"I have something to tell you."

Long-term survivor Regan Hofmann chose that title for her memoir, recounting how she shared her HIV diagnosis with family, friends, lovers and ultimately the world. But some of the most compelling stories were about her mother's response, both to the initial diagnosis and in reaction to Hoffmann's choices as her health took a turn for the better.

Mothers know full well what it's like when their child hesitantly approaches them with this opening remark, "I have something to tell you." It's almost always followed by bad news: I wrecked the car, I flunked my chemistry test, I broke your favorite dish. But for too many, that sentence uttered by their son or daughter was followed by an unimaginable explanation:

"I have AIDS."

For Hofmann, that day came three months after her diagnosis. Living alone in Atlanta, she'd withdrawn from the world, struggling to understand what was happening to her. Finally, recognizing she could not cope alone, she used a weekend visit from her mother to face her fear of rejection and tell her face-to-face.

She said nothing, did nothing, for a minute or two. She stared into space, despondent as a wild animal that's been caught - and knows it will never get away. My heart throbbed in my chest; I could hear it swell and deflate ominously. Then a primal sound came from her mouth - the roaring wail of a mother lioness discovering her slain cub lying mutilated in the grass. It was an awful blend of wrenching agony and fear and emptiness and futility. A sound that said the things there are no words to describe. She pales as though blood was being wrung from her heart. I sat before her, feeling as if I was present at the discovery of my own dead body. She started breathing heavily. Her eyes were wide and dry. She didn't look at me for a while...Then her face crumpled. And the tears came. [2]

Hofmann comforted her mother, holding her as she wailed, assuring her that she would continue to live her life to the fullest. She tried to share details, but her mother's shock made further conversation impossible. Her mother's sudden insistence on making her flight home to New Jersey left Hofmann feeling abandoned.

The shock of such news, especially the news of an HIV diagnosis in a straight woman, required time to absorb. The following day, back home in New Jersey, Hofmann's mother called her. Having had the chance to share this with her husband, she was now armed with a mother's determination to support her child in whatever way she could.

For Arlene Bubb, the conversation took place on the phone. She asked her son Brian, one of the top tie designers in the country, if he had AIDS and held her breath, praying the answer was no. He answered her question with a question: "What would you say if I told you yes?"

Bubb's response was immediate. "We certainly would love you and take care of you and have you home here with us and do whatever we needed. I mean, you're our son." [3]

While some women chose to participate in helping the AIDS community, too many mothers were often dragged into this world after the diagnosis of their own child. Two such women were Patsy Clarke and Eloise Vaughn.

Few politicians - save Ronald Reagan - did more damage in the early years of the AIDS epidemic than North Carolina Senator Jesse Helms. His long history of opposing civil rights was just a prelude to the war he led against the LGBT community in general and, to a level that bordered on obsession, the AIDS community.

An editorial from *The (Raleigh) News & Observer* called out his hypocrisy with a bit of sarcasm:

> The senator implies that because HIV is spread through risky behavior, AIDS sufferers deserve their fate... But to suggest that AIDS victims have it coming and should be punished with medical neglect is no more acceptable than to begrudge a heart bypass for, say, a 70-year old senator who spent years smoking tobacco and eating barbecue. [4]

Patsy Clarke and Eloise Vaughn both lived in Raleigh, North Carolina but did not know each other. Clarke was a staunch Republican; Vaughn an equally politically active Democrat. Their paths did not cross until a mutual friend recognized what they had in common: Each had a son named Mark. Their sons came out to their mothers as gay and HIV-positive. Both died in the arms of the woman who gave them life.

After that friend arranged an initial phone call, the bereaved mothers then met, seeking another person who could understand their mourning and fury. They started a support group for other mothers who'd lost a child to AIDS. It helped, but only to a point. Then one day Clarke - whose late husband had been a Republican activist and friend of Jesse Helms - read that the senator had been quoted implying that people like her son deserved to die.

Clarke felt she had a chance to convince him through that personal connection to change his stance on AIDS funding and towards the people who were suffering. Clarke was not accustomed to advocating, even for a cause so important to her. But she did.

Her June 5, 1995 letter to the senator recalled her appreciation for Helms's sympathy call after the death of her husband. Then she asked a favor of him: not for increased AIDS funding or a change in his position on homosexuality. Patsy asked only that the senator not "pass judgement on other human beings as 'deserving what they get.'" She was polite but firm in that very Southern way of speaking her mind with respect. She hoped only for compassion from Helms: normal, human compassion. His reply came in the mail two weeks later:

> Dear Patsy,
>
> I hope you will forgive my first-naming you. Having known Harry as I did and having read your poignant letter, I just don't feel like being formal in this response.
>
> I know that Mark's death was devastating to you. As far as homosexuality, the Bible judges it, I do not. I do take the position that there must be some reasonableness in allocation of federal funds for research, treatment, etc. There is no justification for AIDS funding far exceeding that for other killer diseases such as cancer, heart trouble, etc.
>
> And, by the way, the news media have engaged in their usual careless selves by reporting that I am "holding up" the authorizing legislation that includes AIDS funding. One of the homosexual activists sent out a totally erroneous press release (and he knew what he was saying was not true) hoping to cause me problems. He failed. I did file a "notify" request because I have two or three amendments that I intend to offer to restore balance to the spending of the taxpayers' money for research and treatment of various diseases.
>
> I understand the militant homosexuals and they understand me. They climbed onto the roof of Dot's and my house and hoisted a giant canvas condom.

As for Mark, I wish he had not played Russian roulette in his sexual activity. He obviously had a very great deal to offer to the uplifting of his generation. He did not live to do all of the wonderful things that he might otherwise have done.

I have sympathy for him - and for you. But there is no escaping the reality of what happened.

I wish you well always.

Sincerely,

Jesse H. [5]

Clarke was devastated. But his words triggered a response she could not have anticipated. The two widows became activists with a clear goal: defeat Helms. She and Vaughn founded a political action committee (MAJIC: Mothers Against Jesse in Congress) that quickly grew from 30 to over 1,000 members. They did whatever they could: seeking support in gay bars, at church socials and at the Democratic National Convention.

A TV ad created for their campaign so incensed Helms that he threatened to sue stations across North Carolina if they aired it. His influence was such that of the eight stations, only three ran the ad. People magazine profiled the MAJIC mothers. The women did interviews on talk radio stations, taking questions from callers, some of whom were vocal in their condemnation. Hate mail arrived daily, but so did donations.

On election night they gathered at Vaughn's home for the results. Though their efforts fell short, and Helms was re-elected, they had made their fury known to Helms, and the entire state.

Another mother was already an activist when the epidemic struck. Rev. Willie Barrow of Chicago was an icon of the civil rights movement. Her congregation, Vernon Park Church on the south side, was home to many, and the 130 people she mentored – whom she called her godchildren - included a young Barack Obama. Known as the 'Little Warrior' for her diminutive size and feisty demeanor, Barrow had begun activism when she led a demonstration against segregated school buses at the age of 12. She went on to work alongside Rosa Parks and Rev. Dr. Martin Luther King, Jr. on boycotts and sit-ins, including the 1964 March on Washington and the 1965 March on Selma. In the late 1960s, she and Rev. Jesse Jackson established the Chicago chapter of Operation Breadbasket, which become Rainbow PUSH Coalition. Social justice activism was in her blood, as much a part of her life as her joyful faith. But it was for a very personal reason that she became involved in the AIDS community.

Her son, Keith, was a gospel singer who she believed contracted AIDS in the late 1970s. In the absence of real treatment, he died in 1983. Rev. Barrow nursed him and later made one of the first panels of the AIDS Memorial Quilt to honor him. His funeral drew 1,000 people, at a time when many churches refused to bury anyone who died from AIDS. Asked if her relationship with Keith had changed when he told her he was gay, her response was swift and forceful.

Never! If God loved him, I had to love him. If anything, it drew us closer together, because I knew he needed special understanding, special communication. I went out of my way to show I loved him. [6]

Rev. Willie Barrow, NAMES Project AIDS Memorial Quilt display, Navy Pier, Chicago, July, 1988 (Lisa Howe-Ebright)

At the 2015 memorial for veteran Chicago journalist Andrew Patner, activist Lori Cannon remembered the day in 1988 when the AIDS Quilt came to Navy Pier. It was one of the first displays outside of Washington and Rev. Barrow was there.

When the Rev. Willie Barrow came to present her son's quilt panel, it was Andrew who recognized her silent struggle. As a Christian minister, Barrow was challenged to reconcile having a gay son - whose AIDS diagnosis had forced him out of the closet - with her faith. Shell-shocked, she could not bring herself to turn over her son's quilt panel to be incorporated into the display - because it was the final act of saying goodbye. It was Andrew who sat quietly with her for hours and hours, gently rubbing her back, listening to her, comforting her and finally convincing her that it was time to let go. That single act of kindness transformed Willie Barrow into an ally of the LGBT community, which she was until the day she passed. [7]

One of the most famous mothers in the AIDS community was first one of the most famous mothers in the LGBT community: Jeanne Manford of Queens, New York.

Elementary school teacher Jeanne Manford was the mother of Morty, a gay man who was present at the Stonewall Riots, rightly identified as the inciting incident of the LGBT rights movement. He became a member of the Gay Activist Alliance, fighting for civil rights legislation in New York City that included protections for the LGBT community.

At a gathering of political insiders in April 1972, Morty and his fellow activists, protesting media misrepresentation of them, were attacked and beaten. Morty was kicked by the president of a firefighter's union. The police did nothing.

Jeanne Manford was furious and wrote a letter to a local newspaper proclaiming her love for her son and her outrage for his treatment. Suddenly, she and her husband were sought out by the media. Three years after Stonewall, parents who were public supportive of LGBT offspring were still a rarity.

And while this unexpected notoriety changed her life, it was nothing compared to what she did two months later: she marched with her son in the New York City Pride Parade, then called the Christopher Street Liberation Day Parade. She carried a homemade sign that read "Parents of Gays, Unite in Support for our Children." (In the other hand was a shopping bag containing her galoshes, in case it rained that day.) Parade-goers greeted Jeanne and her bold sign with exuberant cheers. That afternoon, Jeanne Manford became the surrogate mother for thousands of disowned gay men.

The following year, 1973, Jeanne assembled about twenty parents for a meeting of what would become Parents, Families and Friends of Lesbians and Gays (PFLAG), an organization currently with more than 400 local and state chapters around the US.

Twenty years after that famed parade, and a few months after her son's death, Manford presented his panel at the international display of the NAMES Project AIDS Memorial Quilt in Washington, DC. Her message:

> Every square of this quilt represents, on its surface, the life of one person lost to the devastating scourge called AIDS. But each also stands for hundreds, thousands of other lives: those of all who loved that person and lost him or her too soon. And while all the sewing, all the sweat and tears, can never mend the hearts and lives ripped apart by this plague - the very existence of the Quilt can give us comfort, because in each square's interdependence on every other square, we see our own need to stand united against AIDS. And, by seeking shelter together under the blanket itself, we can find the warmth and love of all those who have suffered from its horrible, indiscriminate wrath. [8]

Family AIDS Support Network (FASN) was an outgrowth of Circle of Care, a support group for family, friends and caretakers of people with AIDS at Howard Brown Memorial Clinic in Chicago. Betty Stern, whose son's HIV diagnosis was the catalyst for her return to school to earn a master's degree in Human Services Administration, was instrumental in bringing FASN under the auspices of Test Positive Aware Network (TPAN). Organized in 1987, TPAN's mission is to save lives and empower those affected by HIV/AIDS and related illnesses. FASN's membership extended throughout Chicago and the suburbs, with meeting attendance providing information and resources, as well as emotional support.

They seek a place to talk about their pain, to cry about it. Our groups offer a lot of release. [9]

The mothers of children like Ryan White and the Ray brothers of Florida did not have to face homophobia as the boys were heterosexual. But AIDS hysteria targeting them by mobs was just as virulent.

When hemophiliacs began testing positive for HIV, because of tainted blood from the public supply, a worldwide panic ensued. Gay men suddenly were prohibited from donating blood. Hospital patients refused transfusions from the blood bank, not trusting of the safety. The Red Cross, warned repeatedly of the danger in the blood supply, dragged their feet in policy reform, resulting in additional infections. Misinformation abounded - some people even believed donating blood could result in infection. That ban still exists, despite dramatic advanced blood screening, as well as the development of drugs that can lower a viral load to undetectable levels, making transmission impossible.

Louise Ray and her husband, Clifford, lived in Arcadia, Florida. They had four children ranging in age from six to 10. Their three sons, Richard, Robert and Randy, were all hemophiliacs. All were infected with the AIDS virus through contaminated blood-clotting drugs. When neighbors heard of this - and that the boys would still be going to school - they protested, insisting their own children were in danger.

In big cities and small towns around the world, children with AIDS were banned from school. If they were allowed to attend classes, they were forced to use separate bathrooms as well as disposable plates and silverware at lunch. They were not allowed to play sports for fear of an injury that would bleed. Even when

*"I Have AIDS
Please Hug Me", Center for
Attitudinal Healing, 1987*

public health officials met with parents to share the facts, as they did in Arcadia, hysteria usually won out.

The Rays had gone to court to demand that their children be allowed to attend Memorial Elementary School, after having been thrown out. At the beginning of August 1987, a judge ruled that they be allowed back.

The return of Richard, Robert and Randy was met with a walk-out by half the student body. The Rays received threatening phone calls, but Louise refused to take them seriously. She remained focused on supporting her sons and did not believe her neighbors would actually do harm. Three weeks later, somebody proved otherwise; they decided to burn the Ray home to the ground. The only person in the house was Clifford's brother, who escaped with injuries. The community won: the family moved.

In 1994, after pressure from the Rays and other hemophiliacs, the Department of Commerce convened a committee to investigate the negligence surrounding the safety of the nation's blood supply. Not one to seek the spotlight, Louise Ray gave the final, powerful testimony of the nine-hour hearing:

You see the bumper sticker that reads 'Blood, A Gift of Life'? That is such an atrocity. For us, blood was a gift of death. You individuals who sit before us today, you hold the key to our future, one of hope that our country will at long last be protected. Or you hold the key that opens the door of fear that the future generations of hemophiliacs will also be lost to neglect. [10]

Another mother of an HIV-positive child opted to take a more public stand against fear and misinformation on an international level - not only for her son, but for all children infected. Jeanne White-Ginder was the mother of Indiana schoolboy Ryan White, a hemophiliac who had been infected by tainted blood products in 1984. The abuse of White was relentless: the child was banned from attending school, someone shot at their house, and even neighboring merchants treated them like pariahs. But both Jeanne, a Methodist whose fellow parishioners shunned her and her family, and Ryan, a typical kid with a courageous streak, spoke out, attempting to educate people and dispel myths. Their courage and eloquence earned them international support, powered by friendships with singers Michael Jackson and Elton John. Ryan even was the subject of a TV film about his life.

But even after Ryan died at age 18, AIDS ignorance persisted. His grave was vandalized four times, necessitating moving his remains to another cemetery. But Jeanne continued her work in his memory, serving as an AIDS educator and establishing the Ryan White Foundation focused on helping teens with AIDS. She was also prominent in the campaign to establish the Ryan White CARE Act, signed into law just months after her son's death in 1990, which continues to provide federal support for Americans infected with HIV.

It wasn't until 2017 that the over 4,000 hemophiliacs who died from AIDS were memorialized. White-Ginder spoke at the dedication of the Hemophilia Memorial Circle at San Francisco's AIDS Memorial Grove:

We were roundly ignored by both our government and the drug companies that were supposed to help us. We fought fiercely against an epidemic and the stigma and discrimination that came from it. We spoke out about both hemophilia and the resulting HIV infections that were now so intertwined. We vowed to ensure that this never happens on our watch again.

(The Hemophilia Memorial Circle at the National AIDS Memorial) is an essential step forward to recognizing what people in our community have known for decades: that hemophilia needs to be known, seen, and talked about. The ability to gather, remember, and heal is of the utmost importance. [11]

Brent Nicholson Earle maintains that AIDS killed his mother, though she was not HIV-positive. But she gave her life to the movement to stop AIDS.

Marion Nicholson was by his side when her son, a gay man, decided to run around the perimeter of the United States in 1986 to raise AIDS awareness. Or rather, she followed him in a truck every one of the 9,000 miles the seasoned runner trekked. Her motivation was simple:

Who's going to take care of you? Who's going to make sure you eat? [12]

His ambitious project, called The American Run for the End of AIDS (AREA), began in March of that year in his hometown of New York City.

A former teacher, Marion Nicholson was always active in civil rights and social justice issues. With this massive run, her son's passion became hers. In their travels around the country, mother and son brought AIDS awareness to cities and towns, declaring the need for education, compassion and support to a country still deeply in denial about AIDS.

What started out as her desire to support her son's project became something far more personal. The mother-and-son team visited gay bars across the nation, where they unfurled a map of the US, showing their progress and selling merchandise to raise money in partnership with local organizations. In those bars, Marion was approached by gay men and lesbians alike. Seeing this woman devoting herself fully to her son and his project, was not only welcome, but a source of unexpected inspiration for those who lacked the same connection to their parents. Through fundraising events inspired by the run's arrival, AREA helped raise over $300,000 for AIDS education and services in those communities.

The Run ended in New York City on Halloween, 1986. Brent eventually was profiled for his feat by *People* magazine in 1990, as one of its "20 Individuals Who Shaped the 80s," and he and Marion enjoyed a national recognition that they had never expected. Rather than back off from the exposure, Marion leaned in, accompanying her son on educational appearances. A prominent member of the gay dance club community, Brent suffered the loss of hundreds of friends. He was constantly attending funerals and memorial services. A resident of upstate New York, Marion would occasionally venture into the city to join her son for a sad event.

Marion Nicholson and her son
Brent Nicholson Earle, undated

It was 1991 and the deaths were escalating. Brent could tell that the relentless losses were wearing on his mother. But like Brent, she seemed driven by the tragedies, compelled to keep fighting. On one visit to Manhattan, Marion accompanied her son to the theater to see the smash musical *Les Misérables*. Afterwards, she told her son that the show could easily be about the AIDS crisis and the people who rose up to help their fellow citizens against a cruel government.

While Marion dealt with a variety of looming debilitations, she struggled to support her son and keep raising awareness about AIDS. But it was the death of a young friend, Ryan Thomas, a ten-year-old boy who died of AIDS on Thanksgiving, 1991, that proved to be too much for her, as Brent recalled.

"I feel like my hope has died with him."

"Oh, now, Mom, you always have hope!" I didn't get it. It was like (she thought) I was next. [13]

On December 10, Marion Nicholson suffered a heart attack. She insisted to her son that she was fine, and he need not come home to see her until Christmas. After returning home from the hospital, she died on Friday the 13th. Brent was not at her side; he was attending yet another AIDS memorial service in New York City.

In the summer of 1992, eleven years into the epidemic, America had the task of electing a new president. Both the Republicans and Democrats were holding their respective conventions. While the party remained ideologically a study in contrasts, that summer there was an overlapping of priorities. Both conventions showcased a controversial subject - AIDS. Both conventions selected straight, white, privileged women to speak about AIDS because they were both HIV-positive. It was also, ironically, the year that the CDC finally recognized, after years of advocacy from the women of ACT UP and other groups, that women could contract AIDS.

You can debate the optics of this primetime TV choice. Was it a serious attempt to show that AIDS was not a gay disease, but a threat to all? Was it a cynical attempt to use more socially acceptable messengers to deliver a plea for support? After all, both fell into the familiar definition of innocent victims, one (Fisher) having contracted the virus from her husband, the other (Glaser) from a blood transfusion. Regardless, the appearances of Mary Fisher and Elizabeth Glaser brought AIDS into the conversation during a presidential election in a way not previously seen. To be fair, however, Glaser shared the stage with a gay man with AIDS, White House insider Bob Hattoy. The Republicans had no such corollary.

Elizabeth Glaser was known in Hollywood as the wife of actor/director Paul Michael Glaser, best known for his role on TV's *Starsky & Hutch*. Glaser was infected from a transfusion in the early days of the epidemic, after hemorrhaging during the birth of her daughter, Ariel. Four years later, in 1985, she found out she was infected, as was her daughter. Ariel died at the age of six, though her son Jake, infected in *utero,* is alive and well. She did not pass the virus to her husband.

Glaser's speech to the 1992 Democratic convention took place before a sympathetic audience: sympathetic not just to her situation, but the epidemic in general. The Democratic Party platform read:

> We must be united in declaring war on AIDS and HIV disease, implement the recommendations of the National Commission on AIDS and fully fund the Ryan White Care Act; provide targeted and honest prevention campaigns; combat HIV-related discrimination; make drug treatment available for all addicts who seek it; guarantee access to quality care; expand clinical trials for treatments and vaccines; and speed up the FDA drug approval process. [14]

Mary Fisher's speech to the Republican convention offered a different challenge. The epidemic to date had occurred during the terms of two Republican presidents: Ronald Reagan and George H.W. Bush. The 1992 party platform, which also implored that AIDS be treated like any other sexually-transmitted disease (a response to accusations that AIDS funding was being diverted from cancer funding, in particular), included the following moralizing passage:

> This disease also challenges America scientifically. We must succeed in slowing the epidemic's spread. The Administration has thus placed great emphasis on a variety of prevention efforts

to do so. We must recognize, also, that prevention is linked ultimately to personal responsibility and moral behavior. We reject the notion that the distribution of clean needles and condoms are the solution to stopping the spread of AIDS. Education designed to curb the spread of this disease should stress marital fidelity, abstinence, and a drug-free lifestyle. [15]

Fisher's response to that platform was to address it directly:

You are HIV-positive but dare not say it. You have lost loved ones, but you dare not whisper the word AIDS. You weep silently. You grieve alone. I have a message for you. It is not you who should feel shame. It is we - we who tolerate ignorance and practice prejudice, we who have taught you to fear. We must lift our shroud of silence, making it safe for you to reach out for compassion. It is our task to seek safety for our children, not in quiet denial, but in effective action...To the millions who are strong, I issue the plea: Set aside prejudice and politics to make room for compassion and sound policy. [16]

Glaser died in 1994, but the work of the Elizabeth Glaser Pediatric AIDS Foundation continues, to eradicate global AIDS among children. Fisher remains active, as an artist and advocate on an international level. Her work in Africa includes teaching HIV-positive women to create handmade jewelry to be sold online, the profits returned to the women.

In February of 2016, Family First Health, WellSpan Health and York College collaborated to bring panels of the AIDS Quilt to central Pennsylvania to promote National HIV Testing Day, June 27. The announcement in the *York Dispatch* asked the public for requests, so that panels of loved ones could be displayed. Arlene Bubb, the mother who didn't hesitate to support her son when he told her of his HIV diagnosis, now 87 years old, called the reporter immediately. Before she could even describe the panel she'd help make - a self-caricature of her son Brian in a tie - she was told it had already been identified.

It was not the first time Bubb had seen Brian's panel. She'd even traveled to Washington DC for one of the large displays on the National Mall. The incalculable loss of talent on display in every panel haunted her. And though that is obvious to anyone viewing the panels, there's more that she wanted people to remember.

I want them to know that it's still here. AIDS is still here. It hasn't gone away. I'm thankful that people now have been able to get on medication. Know that you can live with this. But be careful. Don't be stupid. (17)

In the spring of 2008, Patsy Clarke was in a Raleigh rehabilitation center, after triple bypass surgery. She thought she didn't know any other patients, until one day she crossed paths with someone she knew very well being wheeled past her: Jesse Helms.

Clarke was sure he didn't recognize her, so she considered introducing herself. She didn't. A few months later, on the occasion of Helms' death, she was asked why. "In the end, I felt very sorry for him."

Fag Hags, Divas and Moms

The Divas

"I ask here and now for the national leadership that is necessary to fully appropriate this bill because I will continue to come and ask for it again and again and again until this is done, and I will not be silenced, and I will not give up and I will not be ignored."-
Elizabeth Taylor, AIDS advocate [1]

Divas have gotten a bad rap. Once a title bestowed on opera soloists of an elevated stature, it came to mean a woman who was selfish, demanding and high-maintenance. Who would willingly admit to that? But the divas in the AIDS community are women easily recognizable: talented, powerful and selfless. They use their power, their celebrity, as Taylor once admitted, "finally, for good." In doing so, they have influenced their influential friends, passionately devoted fans, and the world.

One cannot exaggerate Elizabeth Taylor's importance in the history of the AIDS epidemic. When her film co-star and longtime friend Rock Hudson died in 1985 - for many, the first face of AIDS - she was still grieving the recent death of ex-husband Richard Burton. Then her daughter-in-law, Aileen Getty, revealed her own HIV-positive diagnosis. As would be the pattern over and over again, when AIDS hit close to home, women responded by confronting the peril.

Taylor began by lending her name to the first "Commitment to Life" event held by AIDS Project L.A. (APLA), honoring Betty Ford (Taylor had faced her addictions at the Betty Ford Center). In the tradition of no good deed goes unpunished, Taylor's involvement provoked death threats and a shocking lack of support from entertainment industry friends.

> "I have never had so many no's said to me," she recalls. "They didn't want to come to the evening, didn't want to be associated. Some very big names [said no] ... I realized...that this town - all towns - was basically homophobic, even though without homosexuals there would be no Hollywood, no show business! Yet the industry was turning its back on what it considered a gay disease." [2]

But Taylor did not discourage easily, persisting and finding those who were willing to participate. Her event raised $1.3 million - more money than the Centers for Disease Control (CDC) had spent on the epidemic in its first year.

For the first time, globally recognized movie star Elizabeth Taylor found a higher purpose for her celebrity status. What had been an annoying and frightening burden at times, now became a tool to effect change. She would turn the tables on the public:

> 'When I saw that my fame could help in my fight against AIDS, I thought, bring it on!' she told Liz Smith. 'If people wanted to come to an AIDS event to see whether I was fat or thin, pretty or not, or really had violet eyes, then great, just come. My fame finally made sense to me.' [3]

There was no professional advantage to Taylor's involvement. Many in Hollywood shunned public support for AIDS so as not to jeopardize their careers. So, Taylor stepped into what was an obvious leadership vacuum, as described by Dr. Michael Gottlieb, Rock Hudson's physician and one of the first to report an AIDS case to the CDC. Taylor evolved to define the role of a diva in the AIDS community at a time when few others in entertainment dared take a stand. Gottlieb, one of the first to report an AIDS case to the CDC, described the breadth of the actress's achievement.

Without private fund-raising, AIDS research and education would have stalled in the epidemic's critical first years. And without Elizabeth Taylor leading the charge, private fund-raising would likely have stalled, too.

"I don't think anyone else could have done it," Gottlieb said. "No one had the strength, the celebrity, and the will to do it.

"Someone in a leadership position - a president or first lady - could have told the country: Do the right thing," Gottlieb continued. "And the country would have listened. But no one in power rose to the moral occasion.

"The cause needed a woman at the pinnacle," he explained. "Because openly gay men are not given the respect that they are due. And if a straight man speaks up on a gay issue, his orientation becomes suspect. Elizabeth was perfect for the role. And I think she knew that." [4]

But what exactly did she do? Yes, she allowed her name to be used to promote fundraisers, she made phone calls, she put the squeeze on famous and wealthy friends. Yes, she had a direct line to the world's most powerful people and didn't hesitate to use it. She could've made an impact just signing checks. But Elizabeth Taylor was absolutely tenacious in her quest.

She was hands-on when it counted, because the epidemic was always personal to her. Loved ones were dying.

Taylor visited Hudson regularly at UCLA Medical Center. Consulting with Dr. Gottlieb, Taylor educated herself on what was safe when dealing with a person with AIDS, rather than giving into widespread (and erroneous) fears that HIV was transmissible by either touch or was airborne.

She always showed up on Sundays, arriving as inconspicuously as possible for the most recognizable woman on the planet. These were not photo opportunities for a rabid press corps. Taylor was there to support a man who'd been her friend for decades. Her

Rep. Nancy Pelosi and Elizabeth Taylor,
House Budget Committee on HIV/AIDS funding,
March 6, 1990 (Nancy Pelosi)

willingness to ignore the hysteria of the times was not lost on those in the AIDS community, who now regarded her as their most prominent advocate.

Taylor's activism took her beyond the extravagant AIDS fundraising events that marked the 1980s and 1990s in major cities around the world. They took her to a place rarely visited by entertainers: Capitol Hill.

In a move that reduced congressmen to stammering fans, she testified before political committees. It wasn't just the movie-going public she was educating; she was demanding action from the federal government. As she reminded that congressional panel, "I will not be ignored."

Nor was she ignored. Admittedly, Taylor was a pampered, spoiled and globally worshipped woman. She was not used to being told no. So, Taylor transformed that diva entitlement into something powerful: she simply refused to accept no from men in power who could make a difference in governmental policy concerning AIDS funding and legislation.

Her activism grew. In 1985, Taylor co-founded American Foundation for AIDS Research (amfAR). A remarkably savvy businesswoman, she later began a separate concern, the Elizabeth Taylor AIDS Foundation, initially bankrolling it by photo sales from her 1991 wedding to husband number seven, Larry Fortensky. The operating expenses of the Elizabeth Taylor AIDS Foundation are still fully funded by her estate.

Elizabeth Taylor's achievements were echoed by another woman no less globally recognizable, no less a subject of fascination. But when this woman took a stance against the stigma of AIDS, she shocked the world.

In April 1987, the first exclusively HIV/AIDS unit opened at Middlesex Hospital in London. There to open the unit was Princess Diana.

Members of the British royal family appear at hundreds of charitable events each year. But their involvement is ceremonial: a ribbon-cutting, a short speech. The Princess was defying British fear and hostility towards the AIDS community, a bigotry played out in the merciless Fleet Street tabloids with headlines such as "Britain Threatened by Gay Plague!" She was taking a stand amidst public opinion in which many people supported the forced quarantine of people with HIV.

As a member of the British royal family, Diana was constrained from making public comments about politics. She didn't have the freedom of Elizabeth Taylor to confront government officials. But what Diana did that day stunned the world.

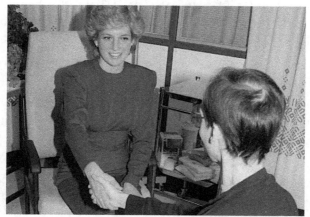

Princess Diana visiting the AIDS Clinic, Middlesex Hospital, London, April, 1987 (Shutterstock)

She shook hands.

She shook hands - no gloves, no hesitation - with one of the patients, a man with AIDS. She did it to prove that the virus could not be passed through casual contact. And she did it because she considered human contact to be a basic right, despite the fear-mongering about AIDS so prevalent in those days. Princess Diana also understood her personal power, as her friend Elton John recalled.

She could walk in a room and make people feel great and that everything was going to be all right. [5]

The media followed her with an obsession not previously seen. Like Elizabeth Taylor, Diana recognized that this was one of the times she was able to use her celebrity for good.

Also like Taylor, her involvement was not limited to photo ops. She was a patron of the National AIDS Trust and the highly influential Terrence Higgins Trust, but also was known to visit the Mildmay HIV hospice.

A short time before her tragic death in 1997, Prince William suggested that his world-famous mother auction off some of her elegant dresses to raise money for the Royal Marsden Hospital Cancer Fund and the AIDS Crisis Trust. Seventy-nine of her cocktail and evening gowns were auctioned at Christie's, raising $3.25 million for the charities.

Elizabeth Taylor and Princess Diana were joined in the battle against AIDS by other famous straight women. Among them were actress-singer Rita Moreno, actress-singer Bette Midler, global phenomenon Madonna, comedienne Joan Rivers and perhaps surprisingly, Debbie Reynolds.

The singer-dancer-actress dubbed "America's Sweetheart," whose marriage to Eddie Fisher was broken up by none other than Elizabeth Taylor, was one of the first Hollywood celebrities to publicly appear at AIDS fundraisers.

On June 23, 1983, she and Shirley MacLaine performed at "An Evening with Debbie Reynolds and Friends" that was described in Randy Shilts' epic chronicle of the early AIDS crisis, *And the Band Played On:*

> The fundraiser for the National KS/AIDS Foundation had all the raciness of a true San Francisco event. When host Debbie Reynolds introduced the surprise guest, actress Shirley MacLaine, with the comment that MacLaine had great legs, MacLaine responded by pulling down the top of her long strapless gown, demonstrating that she had other equipment to match. The crowd cheered enthusiastically: "We love you, Shirley!" Not to be outdone, Reynolds lifted the rear of her slitted gown to reveal her brief black underwear.
>
> "Debbie's 'Tammy' image is blown forever," sighed one realtor in the audience. [6]

The event was not, however, a big moneymaker. Early AIDS fundraising was not reliably successful. At a time when many chose to donate money anonymously, attendance at a public event was a political statement that few wanted to make. Well-heeled donors, accustomed to attending fundraisers for non-controversial causes such as children's charities and the arts, now found themselves approached to support a hot-button issue. Many steered clear of an event where attendance would have personal or business ramifications.

Reynolds' daughter, Carrie Fisher, shared her mother's commitment, working with AIDS Project LA and amfAR. Fisher's involvement went far beyond merely showing up at a glitzy fundraising event. In a 1998 interview, she described her experience as a caregiver in the mid-1980s for her friend, Julian, who she moved into her guest house in his final weeks.

> I would get him manicures and pedicures and he would come outside in his underwear with the catheter...And he was beautiful. He was beautiful. People were freaked out, but this was something I learned from my mother, too. You take care of your own. [7]

Fisher went to battle for Julian against insurance companies that would only pay a nurse to come for half a day. After he died, she had trouble finding a mortuary that would handle his body. Ten years later, another close friend, Michael, was dying of a multitude of AIDS-related infections. Her two-year-old daughter, Billie, had grown close to Michael, so she had to set aside her own grieving to help her daughter navigate unfamiliar feelings.

Another mother-daughter team of HIV charity supporters was Joan and Melissa Rivers. Joan's involvement began in the early 1980s, when she hosted a fundraiser at Studio One, the LA version of New York's uber-trendy Studio 54, to benefit AIDS Project LA. Melissa remembers the death threats her parents received for being involved in this event.

> My parents thought we'd all die together. I was going to school with bodyguards! [8]

Joan's commitment was passionate and wide-ranging. She supported AIDS charities beyond Los Angeles, including amfAR, Gay Men's Health Crisis, Pediatric AIDS Foundation and God's Love We Deliver, where she served on the board of directors for over 25 years. Another diva who was not content to limit her involvement to photo ops and black-tie galas, Rivers was remembered by GLWD after her 2014 death:

> Joan demonstrated deep commitment, compassion and generosity. In 2009, Joan won over $500,000 for God's Love on the NBC reality competition, "Celebrity Apprentice". The final challenge had the contestants putting on a gala, and we remember Joan, getting down on her hands and knees to roll out the red carpet, making sure it was perfect for the event. That's the kind of woman she was - devoted, hardworking, strong and always fighting for what she believed in. Joan volunteered absolutely every Thanksgiving, bringing her daughter Melissa and grandson Cooper with her. Each year, she delivered holiday meals to our clients, surprising them with jokes and their special feasts, bringing warmth and care and brightening

the holiday for so many. [9]

Best known for playing the backstabbing Abby Cunningham-Ewing on *Knots Landing* in the 1980s, Donna Mills remembers the media frenzy that erupted when Rock Hudson's AIDS diagnosis was confirmed. Rock Hudson had recently kissed Linda Evans on an episode of *Dynasty* and the tabloids had a field day speculating that Evans must now be infected. The entertainment industry was far from immune to AIDS hysteria, Mills declared:

> And I do remember people being very scared and people (actors) not wanting to associate with gay people. 'Oh, my God what if I have to do a scene with a gay person and I have to kiss him.' I always thought that was ridiculous. That cannot be the way HIV is transmitted, otherwise everyone would have it. It just didn't make any sense to me. And so, I got on the bandwagon and said, 'that's not the way [HIV is transmitted].' [10]

A long-time supporter of Palm Springs' Desert AIDS Project, Mills remains committed to working towards a cure. When asked at the 2015 Steve Chase Awards how she would describe the theme of the event ("Imagine No AIDS"), she simply replied, "Heavenly."

This rare cadre of courageous divas, at the height of their popularity, took a stand for people with AIDS - all the time mindful of the possible backlash. Reflecting on her participation in the 1985 Hollywood Bowl fundraiser, Rita Moreno recalled:

> To show you how early this was, the press showed up and exclaimed 'Why are you doing this?' The implication being that this could be bad publicity. I answered, 'Why wouldn't I?' [11]

Why did these divas suddenly become warriors? They did share one quality: all of these women had large followings of gay men. Bette Midler's fans went back to the early 70s, when she performed in the gay Continental Baths in New York City. Two of her most iconic songs, "Friends" and "Wind Beneath My Wings" became anthems during the AIDS epidemic. Madonna, who became a prominent fundraiser for amfAR, has always had a large gay fan base.

Despite the courage of these women, Hollywood was still slow to follow in taking a stand against AIDS. Just wearing a red ribbon for AIDS awareness (first seen at the 1991 Tony Awards) was still considered a political act that few were willing to do.

After 1996, though, the urgency towards HIV abated. The new anti-retroviral drug cocktail brought back health and hope to many who had lost both. And while there was no cure in sight, AIDS faded from the public consciousness. Except for World AIDS Day and occasional anniversaries of key events in the epidemic, the leadership and example set by Princess Diana and Elizabeth Taylor were considered no longer necessary.

But there is a new era of show business divas battling AIDS today. It is heartening that these straight women are most often women of color. Their experiences are very different. Not only are they younger than the women who led the way in the 1980s and 1990s, but they live in a world where AIDS was always present.

Actress Kerry Washington, star of ABC-TV's *Scandal*, knew about the virus from an early age:

> I grew up in a progressive household. Both my parents had gay friends - some who were out and some who still aren't out - so I didn't grow up without exposure to gay people, and that was a definitely a gift. At 13 I started working with NiteStar, a theater education program in New York City that came together at the very beginning of the AIDS epidemic. We wrote and performed a show about adolescent issues and sexuality, and as a peer educator I worked closely with people in the LGBT community and alongside LGBT performers. [12]

Taraji P. Henson, the star of the FOX show *Empire*, was one of the women honored by the Black AIDS Institute in 2017 for making heroic contributions to the fight against HIV/AIDS in the black community. At the beginning, the high-risk community was gay men. Now, the demographics have shifted, according to the Black AIDS Institute:

There are about 1.2 million Americans living with HIV today. Nearly 50 percent of them are Black. Of women living with HIV in the U.S., nearly 64 percent are Black. Indeed, experts estimate that 1 in 48 Black women will acquire HIV during her lifetime. Nearly 67 percent of newly diagnosed youth (ages 13-19) in America are Black. [13]

Henson is a native of Washington, DC, which has the highest HIV infection rate in the country. She, too, does not remember a time before AIDS. But she also understands that in the black community, stigma has to be defeated first. For the second time, she's partnering with MAC to raise money through the sale of her Viva Glam products. Unlike many companies that vaguely promise "a portion of the sales" will benefit HIV/AIDS charities, MAC has a history that is difficult to match, donating 100% of the purchase price of those cosmetics. Since 1994, those donations have exceeded $460 million to organizations in 96 countries.

For singer Solange Knowles, the epidemic is deeply personal. An uncle died of AIDS when she was nine. She has been the face of the "Yes, Yes, Yes to Safe Sex" Campaign by the Body Shop and MTV's Staying Alive Foundation. In 2012 she hosted a World AIDS Day brunch that introduced b condoms, developed by African-American entrepreneurs.

Actress Alfre Woodard first entered the world of activism as a vocal advocate in the fight against apartheid. She was a founder of Artists for a Free South Africa. Joined by Danny Glover, Mary Steenburgen and other prominent show business people, she has leveraged her celebrity to lobby for sanctions to force the end of apartheid.

After apartheid ended in 1994, Artists for a Free South Africa was asked by Nelson Mandela, now the president of South Africa, to take on a new challenge: AIDS. The organization was renamed Artists for a New South Africa (ANSA), shifting its mission to open an orphan care program for about 3,500 AIDS children and teens.

When Rae Lewis-Thornton enters a room, all eyes follow her. She holds herself with an unwavering sense of purpose, does not object to being called a diva. In fact, she refers to herself as the "Diva with AIDS".

An Emmy-Award winning AIDS activist, Lewis-Thornton has been featured in countless magazines, national television shows and was a pioneer in using social media to educate and challenge stigma around HIV/AIDS. Her acclaimed blog, Diva Living with AIDS, is syndicated on Body.com, PozMagazine.com and BlackDoctors.com. She has been living with HIV for 35 years and AIDS for 25.

Lewis-Thornton kept her diagnosis a secret for years. She dropped from a size 12 to a size 6, prompting compliments from friends who wanted to know if she was on Jenny Craig. When she did begin to reveal her secret, she was careful to tell friends who didn't know each other, to keep the gossip to a minimum. Her mother initially believed her diagnosis was proof that her daughter was a whore.

At the time, she worked in politics, on the campaign of Chicago's first African-American mayor, Harold Washington. By then, she had already seroconverted. She was ready to go public and decided to do it by telling her boss, the Rev. Jesse Jackson, first.

They were in the kitchen at Jackson's home in on the south side of Chicago when she told him she had something serious to share: "I have AIDS." At first, the civil rights leader was insistent that she only had HIV, because she did not look like she was dying. He knew the difference: he was the first presidential candidate to include AIDS in his platform and recognized the toll it was already taking in the African-American community. His support for Lewis-Thornton was unwavering.

Most conversations are like that: an announcement made quietly, one-on-one. And at first, that's what she did. But in 1994, she announced to the world "I'm young, I'm educated, I'm drug-free and I'm dying of AIDS" on the cover of *Essence* magazine. It was a pivotal moment in the history of the epidemic, for a woman of color to come forward and face the world without shame to help her community.

Rae Lewis-Thornton,
Essence magazine, January,
1994 (photo courtesy of
Rae Lewis-Thornton)

Lewis-Thornton has been open about the challenges of dating, divorced from a man who initially pledged to stay by her. Because of her high profile, any man she dates would have to contend with persistent community of color questions about his sexuality and HIV status. It would be easy to become bitter, but she resists self-pity and continues to dispense AIDS education with optimism and urgency.

The physical challenges have been many, including depression, but Lewis-Thornton has persisted. She has devoted her life to AIDS awareness and education. Today, she is an ordained minister, motivational speaker and advocate. She stands as an example to anyone who quietly despairs. And she is clear on her message.

"I have zero fucks. And that is my secret." [14]

That's an AIDS diva: a woman who will not be deterred by trauma, by disapproval, by bureaucracy, by racism, sexism or homophobia. A woman who will do everything in her considerable personal power to make the world a better place, not for herself, but for millions of people she'll never met - in order to end the epidemic once and for all.

Fag Hags, Divas and Moms

The Fag Hags

I have always identified as part of the gay community. It's been my home since I was in high school and had my first gay friend and went to my first gay bar. It's just where I belonged, where I am happy, whom I feel at home with and where the best music is.
- Nora Burns, Actress and playwright [1]

Fag Hag

Not the most flattering description for a straight woman with gay male friends. The classification is a combination of two slurs.

When the central premise of *When Harry Met Sally* - can men and women 'just' be friends? - is discussed, the caveat is always 'not if they're both straight'. The possibility of a sexual relationship is considered a deal-breaker. And that is why, in the absence of a sexual dynamic, the friendship between a straight woman and a gay man is very common.

Studies conducted on these kinds of friendships focus on cultural similarities: women and gay men have often been powerless and discriminated against. Straight men are a common adversary to both, blocking their quest for full equality in society. Gay men and straight women find a degree of physical and emotional safety in their friendships, in the ability to be themselves without repercussions.

Yolo Akili Robinson is a writer and activist who founded BEAM, a social justice organization whose purpose is to remove barriers to black healing. In demand as a public speaker, he often makes presentations on gay male sexism. In an essay for *The Good Men Project*, he told the following story:

> At a recent presentation, I asked all of the gay male students in the room to raise their hand if in the past week they touched a woman's body without her consent. After a moment of hesitation, all of the hands of the gay men in the room went up. I then asked the same gay men to raise their hand if in the past week they offered a woman unsolicited advice about how to 'improve' her body or her fashion. Once again, after a moment of hesitation, all of the hands in the room went up. [2]

Discussions of consent are typically focused on interactions between straight men and straight women. But gay men, too, are capable of sexual harassment and abuse. Later in Robinson's article, he relates an incident in a gay bar, where a gay man grabbed a straight woman's breasts. When confronted, the man brushed off the woman's objections and insisted, "It's not like I wanted her." Many gay men insist it's impossible for them to be sexist because they are not attracted to women. Popular culture stereotypes will show - from TV's *Will & Grace* to the 1997 film *In & Out* - that gay men feel an inherent right to publicly critique any woman's appearance, wardrobe, and social life.

For some straight women with gay male friends, this feels like no man can be trusted. Others brush it off. But to ignore that it happens ignores the complexity of these friendships and the incidence of misogyny among gay men.

The beginning of the AIDS epidemic tested those friendships in ways not imagined. To be associated with a man who was closeted enough to be socially acceptable was one thing. To be associated with a man who was also dying from a deadly virus was quite another. How strong were the bonds of friendship between gay men and straight women when tested to this degree?

Journalist Trudy Ring's experience with this matter began in 1979 when a close friend came out to her. She soon got to know his friends, some of whom became her friends. They remain best friends four decades later. For her, the term fag hag betrays narrow mindedness.

> I wasn't avoiding straight men and relationships, but I met a lot of gay men, liked them and I wasn't going to reject them as friends because they were gay. [3]

Those friendships, coupled with a desire to support the LGBT community in general, led Ring to volunteer at Chicago House.

At that time, Chicago House provided residential and support services for men and women at three separate locations. One was a hospice for those in the end stages of AIDS. The others were defined as transitional housing, for those still able to live independently. Trudy opted to volunteer in the main office. She had witnessed the pain and loss experienced by the volunteers who worked with residents, and felt she was emotionally capable of only supporting them indirectly. Still, she attended numerous memorial services.

As much as Trudy enjoyed her volunteer time, she had a day job working for a financial magazine. And though most of her coworkers considered themselves somewhat liberal, they weren't above the occasional gay-bashing joke. She called them out on homophobic opinions directed at people she loved, even though her pushback strained their working relationships.

Ring found it impossible to avoid the losses. Ernest Tripp, the volunteer coordinator at Chicago House, died of AIDS complications. There would be more as time passed. Upon receiving a volunteer service award from the organization in 1990, Ring explained that she came to work there because it provided services that might someday be needed by someone she loved. She was right. And for that, she is grateful.

For Ilene Shaw, board member at Design Industries Foundation Fighting AIDS (DIFFA), the losses were so dramatic they've defined her life.

Shaw and her tight-knit group of friends graduated from Parsons School of Design. She was the lone woman in a group of six gay men. They were young, carefree, talented and devoted to each other. They worked together, ate together, traveled together,

Ilene Shaw and Michael Margulies,
undated (photo courtesy of Ilene Shaw)

even lived together. By 2001, all the men had died from AIDS. Her closest friend, Michael, was the last to go.

> They were such an important part of my life that was just cut away. I lost a lot when I lost them. They taught me so much. I learned more about being a woman from them than anyone else. They taught me how to dress, how to cut my hair, put my makeup on. It was like I was a doll! They were more glamorous, funnier...There was so much talent they didn't know what to do with it. *(4)*

Shaw grew up in Queens, the daughter of a Holocaust survivor. Her family was first exposed to the gay community through her. And though they didn't experience it in the same way, they understood her grief as her six Parsons friends died from this frightening virus.

Shaw also faced her own challenges. At age 24, she was diagnosed with cervical cancer. Thanks to a radical new procedure that replaced hysterectomy, she survived to give birth to a son.

But always, always, the grief Shaw felt was tempered with anger. Anger at the horrific suffering that her friends endured. Anger at the world outside of this community that didn't give a damn that her friends were dying. Anger at the helplessness that was pervasive in those early years. And even in the midst of so much suffering, as she supported her friends on their deathbeds, she wanted to do more. She just didn't know what.

Her friends told her about organizations that they depended on, like ACT UP and Gay Men's Health Crisis (GMHC). She would attend meetings or write checks, but she didn't find a place that fit her skills until1992 with DIFFA. Originally founded in 1984 as a local organization of designers committed to addressing the epidemic, DIFFA quickly expanded nationally with chapters in Chicago, Dallas, San Francisco and the Pacific Northwest. They've raised over $43 million for AIDS-related programs and organizations around the country.

With her friend and designer, Donald Ruddy, Shaw started working with them on 'A Hundred Legends: A Compilation of Artwork made by people with AIDS', a book that raised money for the organization with windows displays at Barnes New York.

Today, Shaw has realized a dream change in her career: Shaw & Co., producing such spectacular events as Design Pavilion, a 12-day experiential event in Times Square that attracts millions of visitors. But all these years later, she still senses her missing friends' presence - especially Michael's.

> I feel the power of my friends, energized and determined because I want to do it for them. Every single day. I talk to Michael all the time. He died 18 years ago and it's like yesterday. I know he'd look at me right now and say, 'What the hell's wrong with your hair?' (5)

Her passion now is educating her son and his friends on HIV prevention. She wants their generation to know the truth about AIDS, that the epidemic is not over.

Nora Burns is a ball of energy, a tall lithe dancer and comedienne. A straight woman, she has been a mainstay on Manhattan's gay scene for almost four decades, as well as an activist for AIDS issues. Nora met her best friend, David, in Boston when they were both 17. They bonded over disco music and dancing on speakers in gay club, and moved together to New York, where she supported David's exploration as a newly-out gay man. When the friends turned 31

Nora and David in the kitchen, undated
(photo courtesy of Nora Burns)

in 1993, David died of AIDS. Nora mourned her friend deeply. At least she thought she did.

On the anniversary of David's birthday in 2015, what Burns refers to as her PTSD surfaced with a vengeance. The loss of her best friend hit her as if it had just happened, plunging her into a deep depression. The intensity of it took her by surprise. She couldn't understand why, over twenty years later, she felt the grief on such a visceral level. She discussed the matter with other friends who admitted a similar phenomenon but reminded Nora that everyone was too busy as activists or caring for friends back then to really, deeply process death. So, the fallout was happening decades later.

As a way of working through it, both as therapy and art, Nora wrote and then performed *David's Friend*, a one-woman show about AIDS, loss, love and disco, in New York City and other cities. She explained in the show program:

> I've thought long and hard how I could transform this aching sadness and longing for my friend David into a tribute to him, to our friendship, to our past. Then I recalled a note he once wrote me: it ended with "We have great subject matter for a

best seller, shall we make it a collaboration?" I suddenly knew how to honor David's memory: By recounting the wild saga of two kids caught up in the sexy swirl of a never-ending party. The world has changed. So have I. But David remains the same in my memory. It's that David I memorialize. [6]

Author Julia Glass lived in New York City from 1980 to 2004. Her novels are rooted in those years. She's had gay male friends since grade school and dated a few who had not yet come out. Her connection to them is not something easily defined.

Recently, on a questionnaire, I was asked to choose my gender from a dozen options. I saw one I'd never seen before: 'two spirit'. I found out that it's a term unique to Native Americans, but you know what? That's just how I feel: of two spirits, straight woman/gay man. I'm grateful that my very hetero husband isn't threatened. He's a fan of the *Alien* movies, and we've joked that perhaps one day a fully formed gay guy - picture Rupert Everett - will pop out of my chest. [7]

The 1997 romantic comedy *My Best Friend's Wedding* centers around a straight woman, Julianne (played by Julia Roberts) who made a pact with her former boyfriend and straight best friend, Michael (Dermot Mulroney) to get married if they were still single by age 28. When he announces several days before her birthday that he is indeed getting married – but to a 20-year old college student – she decides to break up the happy couple. Her quest requires the assistance of her gay best friend, George (the aforementioned Rupert Everett). Like many rom-coms, the plot line borders on absurd. The friendship between Julianne and George, though stereotypical in many ways, is revealed to be stronger and healthier than the other one. Relieved of the angst of unrealistic expectations, they are brutally honest and unfailingly loyal.

The final line in the movie is spoken by George to Julianne, as a way of soothing her pain and putting things in perspective. It's an accurate description of many friendships between straight women and their gay best friends, acknowledging the limitations while celebrating the joy:

> "Maybe there won't be marriage, maybe there won't be sex, but by God there will be dancing!" [8]

The Fictional Women

"And there was something else I couldn't admit...even to myself: you were gonna die, Mouse, and I couldn't...this is so awful..."
She was pressing her fingertips under her eyes, the way well-bred ladies do to stop their tears. "I couldn't bear the thought of watching you die the way Jon did. I couldn't do that again. Not with you, Mouse. I couldn't bear the thought of...that horror."
- Mary Ann Singleton, Michael Tolliver Lives [1]

Let's face it: few people willingly watch documentaries. They don't always turn on the news for the purpose of learning something new, even if it directly impacts them. In order to educate the public about HIV/AIDS, writers needed to come up with ways to entertain while educating. Lives were at stake; they still are. But until and unless the viewer/reader/listener could identify with the story, they were unlikely to take it to heart.

TV began to address the epidemic early on. *An Early Frost* (1985), starring Aidan Quinn as a gay lawyer coping with his diagnosis, and helmed by openly gay director John Erman, was the first made-for-TV movie to address the epidemic. The following year, the first episodic TV series to include a storyline involving an HIV-positive character were *St. Elsewhere* and *Hill Street Blues*. In the former, it was the diagnosis and death of straight, single Dr. Bobby Caldwell. In the latter, a gay male prostitute is dying.

Like everything else about the AIDS epidemic, the face of AIDS on TV and in film has tended to be a dying white, gay man. Depictions of straight women have typically been limited to portrayals of saintly mothers who overcame their initial revulsion at learning their son was gay, only to rally as caregivers on death watch.

Soap opera fans know that daytime drama writers have always tackled controversial issues. With an overwhelmingly female audience, they have opened national conversations on domestic violence, substance abuse and mental illness. These were all issues with stigma, crises that affected women every day, but were not everyday topics of conversation. As it became increasingly clear that heterosexual women were at risk for HIV, soap operas around the world began to tackle the subject while also educating their audiences. They went beyond the basics of how to avoid infection and addressed how to live a healthy life if you were HIV-positive.

In 1992, a minister in a story arc on the daytime drama *One Life to Live* displayed a portion of the AIDS Quilt. A year later, June 21, 1993, TV observed the first Day of Compassion, where HIV/AIDS-related stories were broadcast on fourteen daytime soap operas and talk shows. By 1997, that number had grown to 200 programs.

There was, inevitably, opposition to this humanitarian effort. At the Daytime Emmys earlier that year, actress Deidre Hall refused to wear a red ribbon, referring to it as a "90s brand of McCarthyism." Still, the effects of this TV consciousness-raising among housewives were distinctly measurable. After the 1995 Day of Compassion, one AIDS hotline registered a 700% increase in calls.

While public service announcements on niche cable channels such as Black Entertainment Television and Univision can increase basic awareness for hot-button issues, it's far more effective when the message comes through the storyline. It's easier for audiences to identify with fictional women who are facing a challenge that could affect them, too. This approach proved true not just in the US but around the world.

In India, the national television service Doorarshan worked with the National AIDS Organization (NACO) and the BBC World Service Trust to launch the first mass media AIDS Awareness campaign in 2002. They chose two popular series, *Jasoon Detective Vijay*

Screenshot of Haath se Haath Millaa,
Indian 'youth reality' TV show, undated

(Best Thriller Series, 2003 Indian Television Awards) and a weekly youth variety show, *Haath se Haath Milaa (Let's Join Hands)*. Follow-up indicated that an astounding 85% of survey respondents learned something new about HIV/AIDS and almost one-third discussed that information with friends.

In Japan, the national television network, NHK, produced *Kamisama Mo Sukoshidake (Please God, Just a Little More Time)*. The storyline focused on heterosexual transmission: a young schoolgirl who became a sex worker and then HIV-positive. The number of HIV tests and counseling requests more than doubled during the run of the show.

The key to reaching HIV-vulnerable audiences of women, particularly young women, in this way is targeting the most effective TV program and creating an AIDS-themed storyline. In Nicaragua, that's *Sexto Sentido (Sixth Sense)*, a so-called 'social soap opera' that routinely covers issues such as sexuality, rape, substance abuse and domestic violence, reaching 80% of 13-17 year olds.

Some soap operas, like other media, stuck with stereotypes: storylines that focused on a gay man infected with AIDS, and whose death would write him off the show within weeks. In the UK, one soap opera told a very different story.

For heterosexual women who have passed menopause and are no longer concerned about unplanned pregnancies, safe sex seems like a concern of the past. Nonetheless, sexually transmitted infections are on the rise for the over-50 group. According to the CDC, 17% of new HIV infections are in people over the age of 50. Of that group, 23% are heterosexual women. That was the audience the UK soap opera, *Emmerdale*, wanted to reach.

Val was a formidable character on *Emmerdale*: strong-willed and often given comedic storylines. Away from her husband on a holiday in Portugal, Val has a fling. She plans to keep the dalliance a secret until her holiday partner contacts Val to reveal that he is HIV-positive. Now she has to confess to her husband her indiscretion and insist that they both be tested. Their results - he was not infected, she was - gave the soap opera a historic first in 2014: an ongoing storyline about a middle-aged serodiscordant couple.

The information about HIV shared in the *Emmerdale* storyline was not new to series producer Kate Oates, but it was to others on the show:

> One of the reasons I wanted to do this story was because I was shocked how ill-informed a lot of people are on this subject. For example, very few of our writers had heard about PEP (Post-Exposure Prophylaxis) ...I've been shocked to learn the extent of the stigmas that still exist around the issue, as they are usually so very wide off the mark. Although I like to think I'm reasonably well-informed, I am sure I will learn more about this subject as we continue with the research, and also learn through Charlie's performance. [2]

Charlie Hardwick, the actress who had already played Val for ten years, enthusiastically embraced the message. She became a vocal advocate of women taking charge of their sexual lives by carrying their own condoms rather than relying on the man, going so far as to hand them out during interviews about the show. A loyal [English] football fan, she found out at one of the games that some viewers couldn't separate her from her character.

I had a conversation with one of the fellas I see at football. I am a season-ticket holder at Newcastle, so you get to know the people around you.

I was going up the steps and I said, 'How are you doing?' and he went, "Woah, woah...don't touch us. I might catch it!'

I gave him a proper talking to.

I said, 'You don't get HIV from touching somebody - you get it from having unprotected sex and that's not going to happen, is it kiddo?' and he meekly said 'no'. [3]

Linda Bloodworth-Thomason, the creator of the hit show *Designing Women*, which aired on CBS-TV from 1986-1993, lost her mother to AIDS, contracted from a blood transfusion.

The award-winning comedy centered around four women in an interior decorating firm in Atlanta. An October 1987, episode entitled "All The Right People" involved a long-time friend, 24-year old Kendall Dobbs, who asked the four women to design his funeral. He was dying of AIDS and wanted the room at the funeral home to be decorated so others who did not have friends, family or financial means, could have a dignified funeral. Bloodworth-Thomason admitted that the title of the episode came from a comment she had overheard in a doctor's waiting room: "The good thing about AIDS is that it's killing all the right people."

The Emmy-nominated episode made clear, unemotional points about the facts as they were known at the time, mostly without being preachy. And it included a memorable confrontation between character Julia Sugarbaker, played by Dixie Carter, and a holier-than-thou client who used the phrase Bloodworth-Thomason had heard, insisting that people with AIDS got what was coming to them. In her patented steel magnolia style, Sugarbaker put the client in her place.

"I've known you for 27 years and all I can say is if God was giving out sexually-transmitted diseases to people as punishment for sinning, you would be at the free clinic all the time." [4]

That one episode, which included a related storyline about Mary Jo appealing to the school board to present accurate sex education, represented one of the most effective lessons in HIV and safe sex that could be packed into twenty-two minutes of television.

In 1996, the medical drama series *ER*, brought AIDS into a hospital setting for the first time since *St. Elsewhere*. At Chicago's fictional County Hospital, the husband of physician assistant Jeanie Boulet, played by Gloria Reuben, is admitted and diagnosed HIV-positive. At the time, Boulet was having an affair with Dr. Benton, so she had an AIDS test. The opening episode of the following season reveals that Dr. Benton tested negative, but Boulet was infected. Fearful of losing her job, she keeps her diagnosis a secret from all but Benton. He doesn't break her confidence, but that doesn't stop him from trying to limit her contact with patients, sometimes in unreasonable ways. At the suggestion of a patient in the hospital's AIDS ward, Boulet not only seeks treatment elsewhere, but assumes the cost herself, so her employer and insurance company will not know. That excruciating and expensive decision was a common one in real life for many people who wanted to keep their HIV diagnosis private.

Her story, over the next couple of seasons, was one that was quietly being played out in many places: who to share her diagnosis with, whether to date again after separating from her husband, fear of infecting patients she's working with. Eventually, her status becomes known by her supervisor, Kerry Weaver. Jeanie Boulet, observing strict guidelines (now known as universal precautions) for patient contact, settled back into the everyday life at County Hospital.

After 15 seasons, *ER* ended in 2009. One of the characters brought back for the finale - at the insistence of Reuben - was Jeanie Boulet. During the intervening eight years, the actress became an outspoken advocate for black women with HIV.

I look at these women's faces, and I could see in their eyes that they felt like their stories had been forgotten, that people had forgotten about that issue...that they are nowhere to be seen on television anymore. [5]

One series found an unusual way to focus on AIDS: *The Golden Girls*. The wildly popular comedy about four elderly women living in Florida addressed many serious topics. The writers found ways to address ageism, homophobia, sexism, euthanasia and homelessness with respect and humor, educating their audiences without preaching. In 1990, they managed to find a way to prove that AIDS was a virus that could touch the most unlikely people.

Betty White,
1989 Emmy Awards

The storyline involved a letter Rose received from the hospital after gallbladder surgery: it was a request to come in for an HIV test. Writer Tracy Gamble, like Linda Bloodworth-Thomason was inspired by an experience of her mother's to write the episode "72 Hours". The title refers to the waiting time in 1990 for HIV test results. Today it's possible to receive almost instantaneous results for an HIV test.

My writing partner, Richard Vaczy, and I thought it would be a good storyline for Rose, partly because the audience might view her - and she views herself - as the last person who might have to worry about HIV. After all, she's just a Goody-Two-Shoes from

Minnesota. We also liked how with the four characters, everyone could have a different opinion about the subject, which would be a good way to raise issues we wanted to raise while still being entertaining. So, Rose had the common reaction of thinking, "I've never been bad - why did this happen to me?" She then lashes out and says to Blanche, "You must have gone to bed with hundreds of men. All I had was one innocent operation!" When Blanche responds, "Hey, wait a minute; are you saying this should be me and not you?" it raises questions of what is "good" and what is "bad," and what does it matter, anyway? As Blanche reminds her that AIDS is not a bad person's disease, she's saying that just because I'm promiscuous, that doesn't mean I'm a bad person. [6]

The groundbreaking series *Life Goes On*, which ran from 1989-1993, centered around the Thatcher family of suburban Chicago and tackled issues rarely addressed on a weekly basis. The son was played by Chris Burk, the first actor on a TV series with Down's syndrome. Its earlier seasons' storylines focused on that particular challenge, as well as his many capabilities. But in a dramatic break from previous TV portrayals of the AIDS epidemic, the younger daughter was in love with a young man with HIV.

The character of Jesse McKenna was a rarity on TV at that time: a young, straight man with AIDS. That he and Becca Thatcher were in high school and college allowed the series to explore a number of issues that the couple faced. How far do they take their sexual relationship? How does the rest of the family feel, not just about Jesse, but their daughter's risk of infection? Are their friends worried about Becca? Jesse was actually supposed to die within eight episodes, but the storyline continued, thereby allowing the characters to more deeply explore the impact of AIDS on a young, straight couple.

The episodes asked some tough questions about a straight HIV-negative young woman falling in love with a straight HIV-positive man. Her motivation was constantly questioned. Was she vying for attention? For sainthood? Surely there must be some reason other than normal human chemistry.

The series had already been a landmark for Down's syndrome awareness. Now, it educated audiences on the facts about HIV/AIDS - especially in scenes at the AIDS service center where Jesse worked part-time.

Taking these storyline chances wasn't easy. The show had always been considered a sacrificial lamb, scheduled opposite the juggernaut of *60 Minutes* in the 7:00pm time slot known as 'Family Time'. And while onscreen discussions of Down's syndrome were deemed acceptable, any mention of AIDS and safe sex was a hard sell to network executives.

Becca and Jesse represented something else that was unique on TV at that time, because they showed viewers how a serodiscordant couple could have a normal relationship. People with HIV/AIDS at this point were typically introduced in a storyline when they were already dying. They were mostly white, gay men and the relationships explored were usually limited to their parents and siblings. Few examined heterosexual relationships in the HIV community. But *Life Goes On* did, meaning this epidemic could not be dismissed as happening to someone else.

Made-for-TV movies allowed TV producers and writers to delve deeper into the epidemic than a half-hour sitcom could. The conflicts presented in *An Early Frost* were the kind frequently played out in real life: the pregnant sister refuses to come near her brother for fear of infecting her unborn child; the mother is open and understanding while the father is hostile.

This played out again in 1991's *Our Sons*, which presented an unfortunate class-based bias: Julie Andrews, confident and self-assured, is the enlightened mother who must break down lower-class Ann-Margret's prejudices. Rich mom: good and open-minded. Poor mom: bad and homophobic. Though this was also helmed by John Erman, the overall feel of the earlier film was of a dignified, upper-class gentility. There was nothing subtle in this film's heavy-handed portrayals of lower-class women or gay men.

One of the first times we see a straight woman who is a fag hag on screen was in 1990's *Longtime Companion*, directed by

Norman René, later an AIDS casualty. Mary-Louise Parker's Lisa is the sister of one of the gay characters, a regular in their social circle in both NYC and Fire Island. She's with the gang when the first news of the strange 'gay cancer' is reported by the *New York Times* in July of 1981. She's with them when several in the group fall ill, are hospitalized, and die. She doesn't run away.

The characters in Larry Kramer's classic 1985 play *The Normal Heart* are based on real people and events. The only straight woman in the play - indeed, the only woman - was modeled after a doctor Kramer held in the highest regard. Dr. Linda Laubenstein never read the play, never saw a performance. She was, by all accounts, unhappy with the portrayal. In her opinion, Kramer saw the dramatic advantage of depicting a strong-willed AIDS doctor in a wheelchair. He did not disagree. Kramer renamed the tenacious and passionate woman Dr. Emma Brookner.

Dr. Linda Laubenstein, undated

The wheelchair-bound doctor spends most of the play interacting with Ned Weeks, Kramer's alter-ego, as well as other gay men who are her patients. But late in the second act, she's alone on stage, summoned before a government representative to be told her request for funding has been denied. He blames a very competitive grant process as well as the Reagan-led government's distaste for anything that could interpreted as supportive of homosexuality. The government man makes a severe miscalculation: he praises

Brookner as a pioneer but cautions her that the virus is bigger than just her and her practice. That did not sit well with Brookner, whose fiery response reflects the frustrations of real-life doctors like Laubenstein.

> Well, I'll let you in on a little secret, doctor. You can have it. I didn't want it in the first place. You think it's my good fortune to have the privilege of watching young men die?... How dare you come and judge me? [7]

And while the play is fictionalized, the politics contained therein are not.

> You guys have all the money, call the shots, shut everybody out, and then operate behind closed doors. I am taking care of more victims of this epidemic than anyone in the world. We have more accumulated test results, more data, more frozen blood samples, more experience! How can you not fund my research or invite me to participate in yours? A promising virus has already been discovered - in France. Why are we being told not to cooperate with the French? Just so you can steal a Nobel Prize? [8]

The rage in her final outburst was directed not at the virus itself, but the political and medical apathy that condemned millions. Through the character of Dr. Brookner, Kramer was able to reach a far wider audience than any single doctor about the urgency of challenging the status quo. Her bitter diatribe concludes:

> Your National Institutes of Health received my first request for research money two years ago. It took you one year just to print up application forms. It's taken you two and a half years from my first reported case just to show up here to take a look. The paltry amount of money you are making us beg for - from the four billion dollars you are given each and every year - won't come to anyone until only God knows when. Any way you add all this up, it is an unconscionable delay and has never, never existed in any other health emergency during this

entire century. While something is being passed around that causes death. We are enduring an epidemic of death. Women have been discovered to have it in Africa - where it is clearly transmitted heterosexually. It is only a question of time. We could all be dead before you do anything. You want my patients? Take them! TAKE THEM! (She starts hurling her folders and papers at him, out into space). Just do something for them! You're fucking right. I'm imprecise and unfocused. And you are all idiots! [9]

Straight women have been hard to find in novels dealing with the epidemic, except in the background. By the fourth decade of the epidemic, though, they are beginning to be defined by their survival. They are looking back, decades later, on who they were and what they witnessed. While not infected, they, too, should be considered long-time survivors.

The most famous is Mary Ann Singleton in Armistead Maupin's immensely popular *Tales of the City* series. Initially, she was the least colorful character to reside at 28 Barbary Lane in the San Francisco of the 1970s and 1980s. A naive transplant from Cleveland, determined to make her way, Mary Ann unexpectedly found a home among a largely LGBT group of friends and neighbors.

When the epidemic begins, Singleton deliberately distances herself from it emotionally. She prefers to believe her friends are immune, until they aren't. When her husband admits infidelity and the need for an HIV test, her world is shattered. It's the final straw that pushes her to leave San Francisco for a new job, abandoning him and their daughter. When she returns, she wanders around her old neighborhood, reminiscing, seeing ghosts of those long gone.

The past doesn't catch up with us, she thought. It escapes from us. [10]

The character at the center of Rebecca Makkai's critically-acclaimed *The Great Believers* bridges the storylines of 1985 Chicago and 2015 Paris through the lens of the AIDS epidemic. Barely twenty-one when the book opens, Fiona finds that it takes a different crisis to bring her to Paris to make the connection between those two cities, those two lives.

The Great Believers begins at the memorial service of Fiona's brother, Nico. The alternative ritual was necessary as Nico's friends were not welcome at the church funeral organized by his parents. Fiona is surrounded by his friends and lovers, young gay men who had always accepted her not only as her brother's caregiver, but their friend. In the ensuing years, as many of them become sick and die, she finds herself being a caregiver again, this time to Yale, who has lost his entire group of friends. Visiting him in the AIDS Ward at Illinois Masonic Hospital, she goes into premature labor, and gives birth upstairs from the room where Yale dies before she can return.

Thirty years later, Fiona is still in Chicago, running a resale shop to benefit an AIDS charity. Her baby is a grown woman, estranged from Fiona as Fiona had been estranged from her parents. Having hired a private detective to find Claire, who had been last seen in Paris with a small child, Fiona, heads there. She's staying at her friend Richard's apartment in Paris. He's one of the few characters to bridge the decades with Fiona. Now a renowned photographer, he has kept a chronicle of those years in Chicago: grainy videos made with clunky camcorders, photographs ranging from works of art to fading Polaroids, newspaper clippings of parades and demonstrations, bulletins from endless memorial services. Alone, and only after some time in Paris, she opens the albums Richard had kept all those years. The memories overwhelm her, not for the first time, in much the same way as Mary Ann Singleton experienced them.

Fiona's survivor guilt is as real as any experienced by gay men who have been HIV-positive since the 1980s - or alternatively, those who remained HIV-negative. The rehashing of decisions made and words spoken, agonizing over the results that no one could have predicted, haunts her as it haunts so many in real life. But it is an admission she recalls from years earlier, while in therapy with her ex-husband, that lies at the heart of her challenge to love her daughter and others. And though expressed a little differently by

Mary Ann Singleton, it's the same sentiment.

> It had been her failing with Claire all along - pretending not to love her as much as she did. Trying to steel herself against a broken heart, the way she would with a boyfriend. (The first time she and Damian had gone to couples' therapy, the therapist had finally said, "What are you afraid will happen if you open yourself up to him completely?" And Fiona, already crying, had shouted: "He could die!" It clearly wasn't what the therapist had expected to hear. He hadn't been a very good therapist.) [10]

While this is a fictional portrayal, the guilt that is so difficult to articulate is deeply felt by many straight women who have outlived their friends. Some have been steady in their participation in the AIDS community; others have burned out or escaped the horror for their own self-preservation over the years. Regardless, they share the same issues as other long-term survivors, struggling to make sense of what it all meant and what to do with the gift they've been given. That gift is not just life itself but witnessing. In this way, author Rebecca Makkai finally gave them a voice.

The Activists

*I think the statistics of AIDS are so terrifying, so overwhelming that it
makes you think that I can't act. But actually, you can. You can write
letters, you can activate yourself and other people. You can be aware,
you can educate yourself about it and you can talk about it. And all of
those things are extremely positive, even within your group - of your
family and your friends. Merely raising the issue is a hugely important
social and political act and people mustn't think that just because
they're not shifting the world...every time they pick up a pen. The way,
I think, anything has ever really changed on this planet is through
large groups of very ordinary people saying something finally.*
- Emma Thompson, Actress [1]

One of the truisms of life in the HIV/AIDS community is that
everyone winds up being an activist. Many women found
themselves in that role. For some, it represented a continuation of
political involvement born in the civil rights, anti-war and women's
rights movements. For others, it was new. For all, it was a cause
worth putting their bodies on the front lines, to face off against
police and bureaucrats, to stand up for those who could not stand
up for themselves.

Two days after Larry Kramer gave a powerful speech at the
LGBT Center in New York City in March 1987, 300 people met to
form the AIDS Coalition to Unleash Power (ACT UP). Within a few
years, 147 other loosely-affiliated chapters were formed around the
world.

The organizational structure of ACT UP was such that there
was no one leader. A general meeting was held, with reports from

recognized committees, or affinity groups. Requests for actions were put forth, followed by discussion. Then voice votes were taken. At the beginning of each meeting, time was set aside to acknowledge members who had died or were hospitalized since the last meeting.

It was clear early on that there were members whose focus was targeted: access to drugs and clinical trials, housing discrimination, etc. Though women were prominent group members, the prevailing assumption was that AIDS affected gay men, overwhelmingly middle- and upper-class white gay men. They were a group that was largely unused to any form of discrimination. Their privilege was assumed as a fact of life. So, when they began to experience hostility and discrimination in political, medical and legal systems that ignored their needs as people with AIDS, they were shocked and angry.

Gay men feared slippage - that expanding the focus of ACT UP to include women and people of color, IV-drug users or even hemophiliacs and heterosexuals would redirect group resources away from them. Some clung to the notion that what was initially thought about the virus was true: it was a gay epidemic. Period. And they did not approve of changing the conversation. But neither did the women in ACT UP taken kindly to being an afterthought, not when people's lives were at stake.

The women in ACT UP were not interested in being an afterthought, not when people's lives were at stake.

Women activists had specific, targeted issues, such formidable barriers as the failure of the CDC to recognize that AIDS presented itself differently in women than in men.

At a teach-in led by the Women's Caucus (WC) of ACT UP/LA in November, 1990, men made up half the audience. And while some were there to learn and support, others were not.

With the exception of Don and his lover, "Sam" - two men who worked closely with the WC - ACT UP/LA men at the Teach-in continually asked speakers about gay male issues, and WC members countered by asking questions about women and

AIDS to refocus the discussion. "Anna," a Chicana researcher/ activist in a Southern California-based project looking at heterosexual transmission in Latino couples, was peppered with men's questions as to the sexual lives of the secretly bisexual husbands, the need for the Latino community to have its own "Rock Hudson moment" to focus its awareness on AIDS, the possible sources of HIV infection of a local activist priest who was then ill with (and has since died from) AIDS, whether the Latino community was embarrassed by its "gay problem," and possibilities for educational campaigns on AIDS in the Latino community. Only the WC women - and Don and Sam - focused the discussion back on its intended topic, Latinas with AIDS. [2]

"What Women Want" © 1990, Daniel Sotomayor, artist. Original artwork, ink on vellum, Sotomayor Collection, Lori F. Cannon, Owner. Documentation and Curation Courtesy of The Legacy Project

Not surprisingly, a debate ensued as to whether men should be allowed to attend WC meetings. As is often the case with ACT UP discussions, language was everything: was "allow" a pejorative term? Women's Caucus meetings had been deemed safe spaces for women. Could they continue to be if men were present? And if so, what did that mean for women? Would they feel comfortable discussing specific gynecological issues facing women with AIDS in a room half-filled with men?

They decided on a formal "women-only" structure for their Sunday night meetings, with the men of ACT UP/LA required to petition for membership and be voted in. This, they asserted, gave women control over their ambitious agenda and a safe space in which to discuss it. In reality, because the numbers of women in the Caucus were so small, they knew they could not accomplish much without men. A few months later, men were invited back to help plan a demonstration on prisoner rights.

When any issue involving women and AIDS was raised in the general meetings, there was a tendency for it to be delegated to the WC. And while that may have been appropriate, it also put women's issues in a separate, less-important box. It pushed their concerns to the side, making the visibility of women more difficult. They were still a minority within the larger group.

What those women experienced happened in other ACT UP groups across the country There was an urgent need to focus on specific topics, but at the same time, acknowledge the interconnectedness of each affinity group. It's a discussion that has not been resolved. It continues in ACT UP meetings to this day.

Today there are fewer ACT UP chapters, though they continue to be active. Some fell apart from the internal bickering that seemed to be a hallmark of ACT UP, starting in the mid-90s, as a host of different epidemic priorities were debated among members. Others no longer felt an urgent need for activism once the HAART drugs were introduced in 1996. There followed a period of time where AIDS activism seemed dormant. People on the brink of death were experiencing the "Lazarus Effect" when switched to the antiretroviral cocktail. In general, the virus was no longer an immediate death sentence. Thanks to President George W. Bush's President's Emergency Plan For AIDS Relief (PEPFAR) program, progress in Africa was dramatic and admirable. The urgent need that once powered the group seemed addressed.

Cosmopolitan magazine's infamous January 1988 article by psychiatrist Robert Gould, titled "Reassuring News About AIDS (A Doctor Tells You Why You May Not Be At Risk)" sparked protests on their offices. The article asserted that straight women were not at risk having unprotected sex with an HIV-positive man, especially in the missionary position. Even the US Surgeon General, C. Everett Koop, spoke out against the magazine and the article's author.

Once again, the afflicted were proactive as a group. Instead of relying on media to document the news and inevitably misinterpret it, the community controlled the message by creating their own community access TV and radio shows and recording on clunky camcorders. They were going direct to the public, just as we have now, 30 years later, with YouTube and Twitter.

The first patient to ever sit on a clinical trial committee was a member of ACT UP, Mark Harrington. Today, it is unthinkable that patients would be ignored in the development of new drugs. That patient was a white gay man because in 1990, women and people of color were still excluded from the clinical trials to develop new drugs to fight HIV/AIDS.

As previously mentioned, Gran Fury's "Women don't get AIDS, they just die from it" was one of the movement's most famous posters. More than a pithy slogan, it was the deadly truth. In March 1989, ACT UP began what became a four-year campaign to convince the CDC to change its definition of AIDS to include illnesses that were specific to women and IV-drug users. White gay men were not only the public face of AIDS; they were the medical face of AIDS. And medical policy addressed only their needs and ailments.

In 1990, the anger among AIDS activists seemed to swell. Almost a decade into the epidemic, drug development was not slowing down the virus. People who weren't considered at risk – that is, anyone who was not a gay man, IV drug user or a sex worker - didn't give a damn about the thousands who were dying. The face of the epidemic was still a white, gay man. So was the face of ACT UP.

For over a decade, women were not being diagnosed, not being treated, not being educated, not eligible for clinical trials or disability benefits. One example of how this played out was in Chicago at Cook County Hospital.

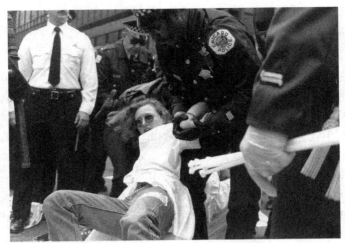

ACT UP Women's Caucus direct action,
City Hall, Chicago, April, 1990 (Linda Miller)

In 1990, Cook County (now Stroger) Hospital was where anyone in the Chicago area with AIDS and no medical insurance wound up being treated. The public hospital, struggling for funding to increase staff and services, was home to an AIDS ward that was bursting at the seams.

With men.

Women still were not being diagnosed with AIDS, often until they were dying or dead, eliminating the possibility of receiving treatments that could have prolonged their lives. At Cook County, those women diagnosed with AIDS were scattered around the hospital. The administration, allowing that there were certainly women who had AIDS, insisted women could not be admitted to the AIDS ward because...there were no women's restrooms. Adding one would cost $1,000 that their present budget simply could not accommodate.

A demonstration attended by activists from around the country and led by ACT UP/Chicago in April 1990, targeted the headquarters of the American Medical Association and insurance companies to criticize their opposition to national health insurance. One group unfurled a banner reading "We Demand Equal Healthcare Now!"

on a balcony of the Cook County building. All worthy causes. But women made sure that women were the focus of this demo, blocking the street with fifteen mattresses representing the fifteen empty beds that could be used create a "women's ward." Well over 100 activists were arrested that day.

The general public was certainly inconvenienced, but the protest worked. Twenty-four hours later, Cook County announced that the money had been found and the AIDS ward would now admit women.

In order to effect change, the women needed a multi-pronged approach. They took their grievances to Washington in October 1990, in front of the Department of Health and Human Services. Many of the women who demonstrated were themselves dying from AIDS, because they'd been diagnosed too late for existing treatments to help them. Eventually, 300 groups across the US signed on to the campaign to force the CDC to change their definition.

Social Security followed the CDC's restrictive definition, which was not a requirement, and resulted in sometimes absurd policies. A man with an oral yeast infection fit the definition; a woman with a vaginal yeast infection did not. Nor did women with other gynecological conditions, such as cervical cancer and chronic pelvic inflammatory disease, because they did not show up in men. At that time, 65% of HIV-infected women died from infections that did not qualify them for disability benefits.

Once the definition was changed in January 1992, things quieted down a bit. But that didn't mean the women quieted down, even in ACT UP.

Nanette Kazaoka has been active in ACT UP/NY since 1989. A soft-spoken, red-haired woman with a physical grace that reflects her time as a dancer, she speaks matter-of-factly about her early days as an activist. At the time that she took part in the Stop the Church action at St. Patrick's Cathedral, she was training to become an occupational therapist. Kazaoka was upfront about her involvement with everyone at school, including her professors and classmates.

When I went into school the next day, after Stop the Church, I was attacked verbally by - who do you think - all the Orthodox Jewish girls that were there. Nobody Catholic said a word. [3]

Her first arrest was at an action targeting then-Presidential candidate Bill Clinton, to bring focus to the need for more AIDS funding. She did not mind getting arrested.

Nanette Kazaoka arrest,
NYC, June 12, 1991
(photo courtesy of Nanette Kazaoka)

Well, that particular time was very pleasant. The fact that the guy (a police officer) took a picture and gave it to me was very... It was fun. It was not bad at all. It was only like three hours. [4]

Despite being arrested multiple times over the years, Kazaoka has never gone to trial. All have been classified 'desk appearances.' Sometimes that meant more than one appearance for each arrest. But any community service requirement was often assigned to Housing Works, the spin-off group from ACT UP that lobbies for better housing for people with AIDS.

For many women, their HIV diagnosis was the start of a life defined by activism. The 2017 documentary *Nothing Without Us: The Women Who Will End AIDS* profiled women activists in Africa and the southern US.

One of the most powerful stories in the film elicits gasps from its audiences. Jeanne Gapiya of Bujumbura, Burundi was an accountant. When she was pregnant in 1987 with her second child, she found out she was HIV-positive. Her doctors urged her to have an abortion because there were no treatments for children born with the virus. She agreed. Her first child and her husband, also HIV-positive, would die within two years. Later, remarried, and determining that her own health was stable, Jeanne wanted to have another child. But she was told that her uterus had been removed during the abortion, without her consent.

Jeanne's birth as an activist came while listening to a sermon condemning people with HIV as sinners. Gapiya found the courage to publicly disclose her status, the first person in Burundi to do so. That courage inspired others to come forward, others who suffered from a lack of comprehensive care. The accountant was now an activist at the head of a national movement.

Jeanne Gapiya-Niyonzima,
undated

In the course of *Nothing Without Us,* Jeanne tells her remarkable story in a matter-of-fact way: smuggling antiretroviral drugs across dangerous borders, pressing her own government to provide free treatment. She continues to serve as president of Association Nationale de Seropositifs (ANSS), the only organization in Burundi addressing the needs of its HIV-positive citizens.

When Andrea Johnson was diagnosed with HIV in 2007, she was already two years into a program she started for at-risk inner-city youth and young adults in Philadelphia: GIRL U CAN DO IT, INC! (GUCDII). Johnson adjusted the mission to include HIV education and awareness, as part of a broader effort to address interconnected issues such as domestic violence, mental health, substance abuse and homelessness. Her passion was born in her own life experience, her desire to move past her initial shame to empower herself and others.

> "I was very naïve, as well as ignorant to how HIV was and wasn't contracted. The man who I acquired HIV from was also my abuser. I had a history of domestic violence, as well as contracted HIV from [being partnered with] one individual, who was ten years my senior and had had the virus for many years before he even met me. In our community, we have a lot of persons of that nature, but at the same time, accountability goes on both ends. I am free and able to talk about it the way I choose because the mistakes that I did make [I know now were] from loving and trusting someone...that I should not have even attempted to love. I use my life as an educational tool to help others." *(5)*

That's how Johnson has not only been able to impact lives through GUCDII, but through its new awareness initiative, Red, White & U HIV Anti-Stigma Photo Shoot and Campaign. She leads the charge to eradicate stigma as a true activist: by living her truth every day.

Activism does not happen in a vacuum. Just like the original members of ACT UP and other groups built on the experiences of women who were part of the equal rights and civil rights

Andrea Johnson, GUCDII (
photo courtesy of Andrea Johnson)

movement, now the AIDS community has a new manifesto, The Atlanta Principles. The stubborn reality of 50,000 new infections in the US every year over the past decade reflects two facts: old strategies have dramatically decreased infections in gay men, but for women and marginalized groups in the southern US, infections have risen.

The risk of infection dropped by more than 90% when HIV-positive partners in serodiscordant heterosexual couples started combination antiretroviral therapy. This is good news that activists struggle to share with the women who need it the most.

Where the 1983 Denver Principles outlined an unprecedented self-empowerment model for people with AIDS, the Atlanta Principles challenges the CDC to take action now. Among their demands:

CDC should work with local officials to develop or improve a local HIV curriculum that educates students about HIV, its treatment and prevention, behavioral and pharmaceutical, and works to counter HIV fear and stigma. CDC should survey students to help ensure the curriculum's effectiveness.

The CDC must be careful to monitor HIV incidence for a new wave of young IDUs (injection drug users) and for women at particular risk.

CDC must focus surveillance of subpopulations living with HIV, including seniors and women, so that the information gathered will improve care. [6]

Anger is a motivating force that cannot be discounted. Throughout the epidemic, the target of that anger has included the government, at all levels; religious institutions; schools; medical researchers and practitioners, as well as employers, landlords, pharmacies and banks. But the anger for the virus itself comes up again and again. It fuels activism like nothing else. In one of her last public statements, New York City's Iris De La Cruz made sure no one misunderstood the motivation for her fiery, eloquent activism.

There are the ditzes who insist that they love this virus because it's a part of them. Tell me this after you've stopped counting the deaths of have spent time with someone suffering from dementia. Let's get this straight: I hate this virus, and it's this hatred and rage that keeps me going. Wimps get buried." [7]

The Artists

"Talent is not replaceable." - Laurie Mallet [1]

Laurie Mallet was president of WilliWear Limited, a company she founded with designer Willi Smith, who died from AIDS in 1987. Like many fashion companies in the 1980's, theirs was not prepared for his death.

The fashion industry lost great talents: Halston, Perry Ellis, Willi Smith. Not only the creative forces whose names were on the labels, those who made the garments, sold them, designed the store displays. An entire industry.

Few professions were hit as hard by the AIDS epidemic as the arts. Theater, film, music, dance, visual arts, design, fashion: all were decimated by the loss of established talents and those just beginning to emerge. And while it's an exaggeration to insist that an entire generation was lost, the contributions of those whose careers were cut short certainly affected those who followed. And though the losses that immediately come to mind tend to be gay men, the careers and lives of straight women were also cut short.

Those deaths were visible, but as Colleen Dewhurst pointed out in the Introduction, they were not limited to professions that traditionally included a large number of gay men. The deaths were everywhere. Still, it took the losses of prominent men and women, considered stars and admired by millions, to awaken an America in denial.

By 1989, the world was beginning to realize that gay men were not the only ones at risk of infection. But few were prepared for the news that actress Amanda Blake, who became famous for her portrayal of Miss Kitty on the classic western TV series *Gunsmoke*, died at 60 from cytomegalovirus (CMV) hepatitis. The AIDS-related form of hepatitis was believed to the result of infection from her husband, Mark Spaeth, who died of AIDS complications in 1985.

Blake kept her diagnosis private because she feared that attention from the tabloids would adversely affect her work with animal welfare groups. As far as anyone knew, she had oral cancer. Her doctor was allowed to reveal the truth only after she died.

She was everything these exotic gay men were not. She was one of those actresses who was familiar and safe. Her personal life was not a subject of tabloid gossip. She was not in a designated high-risk group. The decision to disclose her true diagnosis - a right that everyone should have - was hers. But that desire for privacy is not without its critics.

Fans of Israeli singer Ofra Haza kept a 13-day vigil outside her hospital in February of 2000, where she was dying from what they thought was organ failure. It was, in fact, AIDS.

Ofra Haza, unattributed, 1994

Haza was an international superstar, a Yemeni Jew whose story of rising from poverty to stardom inspired many. "The Madonna of the East" won second place in the 1983 Eurovision song contest and performed at the Nobel Prize ceremony honoring the Israeli-Palestinian peace process. She sang the role of Moses' mother in the animated film *Prince of Egypt*. But despite the devotion of her fan base, she did not want them to know the truth. Most of the hospital staff didn't know, either, a fact that led to fear and resentment later. Her doctors and family respected her wishes. They were not the ones who disclosed the news. It was the press.

Tabloids were still going wild over the possibility that famous people had AIDS, but it wasn't a tabloid that broke the news. In fact, it was not announced in a sensationalistic manner because it came from a trusted source: Haaretz, the longest-running print newspaper in Israel.

A debate raged as to the ethics of that outing. Many believed that the stigma around HIV and AIDS needed to be addressed and defused; in other words, good could come from this news. Others believed she had been betrayed, that her wishes should have been honored even after her death. And though the controversy made AIDS a topic of conversation throughout Israel, doubling calls to AIDS testing sites in that country, it did not end the debate over who had the right to disclose a diagnosis.

There was no debate for American poet Tory Dent. She did not shy away from writing about the virus that killed her in December 2005 at the age of 47. In fact, she felt it intensified her need to write.

Not focused on whether her poetry would survive her, she nonetheless worked with the Estate Project for Artists with AIDS. Founded in 1991, they advised artists on estate planning, assisting in writing wills and helping choose trustees. She considered the ability to make these plans one of the advantages of testing early. In giving her a measure of control, she admitted, "If I can survive the emotions caused by HIV, I can survive the events, too." [2]

In *HIV, Mon Amour*, Dent's poetry collection that won the 1999 James Laughlin Award of the Academy of American Poets, she faced her fears head-on.

> Many rivers to cross,
> And it's only my will that keeps me alive,
>
> As if I had crossed many rivers already;
> Somnambulistically treading the currents, Christ-like, with bare Feet,
> Both vulnerable and omnipotent,
> Both the protagonist and bird's eye voyeur of the protagonist
> Deep inside the beautiful, omniscient double vision of my sleep.
> I awake, soaked in sweat, panting from the droves of dead bodies
> That awaited me on the other side of the riverbank.
>
> I've been licked, washed up for years
> Like a slave collared and leashed by my way.
>
> For in my heart of hearts I know that probably I'm dying.
> For in my heart of hearts I know that I'm going to survive.
>
> How I know this exactly splits my skull in half with a chisel,
> No longer human, the hemispheres of my brain have turned to Marble,
> A Modernist material born like a runt, a last resort
> From the supplemented content of my thoughts, i.e., my "pride." [3]

Poet and essayist Adrienne Rich spoke of the importance of the poetry Dent wrote after her diagnosis seventeen years earlier.

> She teaches us that poetry not only is not equal to but must speak out of extremity and that in all extremity - AIDS, disasters, human disasters such as we're seeing around us constantly -

that silence, if it's not death, it is defeat. (4)

The straight women in the arts who were left behind, those HIV-positive and HIV-negative, used their talents to support their friends and colleagues, sometimes altering their own careers to continue that fight.

Valerie Lau-Kee Lai began volunteering for Broadway Cares in 2003. She has stage managed such Broadway musicals as *Carousel*, *Mary Poppins*, *AIDA* and *Spiderman: Turn off the Dark*, and has served as BCEFA's Producing Director since 2013. Valerie graduated from Brown University in 1986, so her professional career began when AIDS was beginning to take its toll on professional theater. It was hard for a young woman to break in anyway, but the losses and silence made it harder.

> It was something that people knew about, but it happened so fast, people were gone so fast, it was not an environment where you developed close relationships with people unless you were on a show together. I was at the junction where most friendships were mostly from school, not work. By the time you develop a close relationship, the show is over...so very isolating. (5)

When she went on the road with a touring company of *The King and I*, she assisted a stage manager who had AIDS, though he did not talk about it. And she admits she was too young to know how to ask.

> It was difficult for him physically. He was progressing - which I didn't understand - it was late enough that there were enormously expensive cocktails. None of it came without incredible cost - money - and the cost of physical endurance. I didn't ask because I thought he'd explain, offer, but he didn't...I was blind to so many things. (6)

Now Valerie helps Broadway Cares produce events that routinely raise hundreds of thousands of dollars - even millions - in a single night and keeps pushing the message that everyone needs to hear.

*Valerie Lau-Kee Lai, Broadway Cares/Equity
Fights AIDS, undated*

You have to take care of yourself, know your status, being open, being smart. It's important, the new awareness. We have to remove the stigma. [7]

Another long-time staff member at Broadway Cares is Denise Roberts Hurlin, co-founder with Hernando Cortez of Dancers Responding to AIDS, now a program of BCEFA, in 1991. They were members of the Paul Taylor Dance Company, and like many groups of friends who gathered to create AIDS-service organizations, they gathered with other dancers to figure out how to respond the epidemic that was taking a toll on the dance world.

Before her 1992 marriage to Broadway Cares production manager Nathan Hurlin, Hurlin didn't know a lot of 'average' men who understood her profession or her passion for helping fellow dancers with AIDS. With gay members on both sides of the family, there was nothing to justify.

Dancers faced the epidemic in ways that singers and actors did not. They did not communicate with others onstage with words or lyrics; their performances demand that they be in close physical contact with other dancers. So early concerns about transmission

Tom Viola and Denise Roberts Hurlin,
2017 Fire Island Dance Festival
(Daniel Paul Roberts)

were more of an issue for them than for other performers. "They were there and then they were gone," Hurlin recalls. Like many people, she remembers that loss of contact in those days was assumed to be because that person had died. Even now, she's occasionally surprised to find people alive and well on Facebook.

Today, Hurlin oversees such events as the Fire Island Dance Festival, an annual event that set a fundraising record in 2018 for the sixth year in a row, raising over $600,000 on one summer weekend. She sees in the younger dancers a surprising but inevitable difference from the early days: They've grown up in a world where AIDS has always existed, but without the intense personal connections.

And while it would be disrespectful to say that they do not share her passion for ending the epidemic and supporting those with the virus, it is a truth that many straight women in the AIDS community deal with every day. The state of the epidemic has improved, but people are still in need, and as Hurlin reminds us, "We're still here to help". [8]

The Caregivers

"Underneath my anger is anguish and pain from watching my brother's health deteriorate, dealing with my anxiety over his precarious health, and watching him struggle to fulfill his dreams and goals...Tad wants to feel he's making a difference, an impact. I want him to know that in my life, he has." - Jennifer Miller [1]

An ongoing stereotype in the history of the AIDS epidemic has been that straight women - in fact, women in general - were mostly caregivers. Untrained as medical professionals, they took care of their friends and volunteered in hospices or other settings. They were the ones delivering meals, transporting people to doctor's appointments, visiting them in the hospital, tending to personal needs. They stepped up to fill these needs and more.

Jennifer Miller expressed the painful challenges family members faced when taking care of someone with AIDS. She watched her brother Tad deteriorate in 1992, helpless to control the disease or his suffering.

First, I tried to control the diagnosis: "Tad is HIV positive, but he won't develop AIDS." That didn't work.

Then I tried to control who knew about Tad's illness. Initially I told only my husband. Then, unable to contain this secret, I told people at work. No one mentioned it again. This lack of response was not atypical, but I felt emotionally abandoned and ignored.

I also tried to control Tad. I tried to tell him what to feel. When Tad was scared and angry, I'd reassure him of people's good intentions and human decency.

Now, not only do I understand Tad's feelings, I experience them as well. [2]

Anger is a common theme in the AIDS epidemic. "United in anger" is part of the ACT UP slogan. Miller's anger - at the virus, at her coworkers, at herself, at the world - fueled her as it fueled many. The lack of control she felt was shared by everyone from medical professionals to family caregivers.

Another woman who struggled with how to support a sibling was Connie Kiosse. Her younger sister, Christine, experienced a harder life beginning with an arranged marriage at 15. One struggle after another, though not including drugs or alcohol, culminated in the shocking news that her baby sister was HIV-positive.

Kiosse didn't know how to arrange her emotions, including anger at the man who was responsible, in order to understand Christine's new life. It was an ongoing challenge to allow her sister to maintain control over what time she had left, to not rush in to override her decisions. There were hits and misses. One, in retrospect, was the decision to go to a movie: Boys on the Side, starring Whoopi Goldberg, Mary-Louise Parker and Drew Barrymore. She wasn't sure why she took her sister to a movie about a straight woman dying of AIDS: was it an attempt to share the experience?

Several years after Christine died in 1999, Kiosse watched the film again, this time at home and alone. And as expected, she watched it differently this time, wondering what her sister was thinking when they sat in that darkened movie house on the north side of Chicago. Did Christine see her future?

But now when she watched it, instead of the pain and inevitability of loss, she saw three women living life, loving life. When the credits rolled, and the song "You Got It" by Roy Orbison played with the words "anything you want, you've got it", it made her cry. Because that was what she'd tried to do for Christine: give her anything she wanted.

There is one woman who, for many in the HIV community, stands out. The roles she filled were often filled by straight women, but rarely by one alone. The challenges faced by 'The Cemetery Angel' were common in the early years of the epidemic, and becoming common again in many places. Her example makes her unique.

In 1984, twenty-five year old Ruth Coker Burks was spending a lot of time at University Hospital in Little Rock, Arkansas with a friend who required multiple cancer surgeries. She couldn't help but notice one room, its door covered with a big red bag. She overheard nurses bargaining to avoid going into the room.

In the early days of the epidemic, when hysteria overcame the few facts already known, isolation was the default treatment of people with AIDS. Some hospitals delayed assigning rooms, because the record of admitting people with AIDS could affect them negatively: no one wanted to deal with the public relations challenges of being known as an "AIDS hospital". If patients died in the hallways - not uncommon - before being admitted, that was acceptable. Because they wouldn't count.

There's no question that medical personnel had to deal with the risk of infection every day. Universal precautions - something we now take for granted - were introduced to protect workers. But because so little was known at the beginning, many hospitals went overboard. Staff and visitors were required to wear hospital gowns, masks and gloves. Eating utensils were disposed of. Bed linens were burned. Every surface was cleaned with bleach. Fear was harder to erase.

It worth noting, too, that many people did not understand the difference between 'infectious' and 'contagious'. It's an important distinction that still requires explanation. The virus contains a risk for those exposed through unprotected sex, contaminated blood products and IV drug use. It poses no threat to anyone via a sneeze, a kiss, a cough, tears or handshakes. But people clung to their fears. They regarded the constant updating of information in those early years, as the facts became known, as suspect. It was easier to avoid all contact with anyone who had the virus than to accept that medical knowledge was evolving.

Burks was already educated about the epidemic because of her initial concerns about a gay cousin who lived in Hawaii. She believes now that some higher power moved her to walk into that room. Alone in the room was a young man, who had shriveled to less than 100 pounds. He told her he wanted to see his mother.

She went to the nurses' desk to tell them what he said. After their initial shock that she'd gone into his room, they laughed. "Nobody's coming. Nobody's been here, and nobody's coming." Unable to let it drop, she called the young man's mother, who promptly hung up on her.

> "I called her back," Burks said. "I said, 'If you hang up on me again, I will put your son's obituary in your hometown newspaper and I will list his cause of death.' Then I had her attention." (3)

Her plea, from one mother to another, fell on deaf ears. He was already dead to his mother because he chose a sinful lifestyle. It was the first of many conversations she would have over the years with families of over 1,000 people dying from AIDS. The overwhelming majority felt the same way as this mother.

What she did next, more so than walking into his room or making that phone call, changed her life. Until then, she was simply trying to help. But when she walked back into his room, her new role was defined.

> "I went back in his room," she said, "and when I walked in, he said, 'Oh, momma. I knew you'd come,' and then he lifted his hand. And what was I going to do? What was I going to do? So I took his hand. I said, 'I'm here, honey. I'm here.'" (4)

'I took his hand.'

As shown by Princess Diana when she visited the AIDS ward in London, few things had more power in 1984 than the willingness of anyone - friend, family, nurse, stranger - to touch a person with

Ruth Coker Burks (photo by Brian Chilson)

AIDS. Even in those early days, casual contact had been proven to be risk-free. But paranoia and fear still reigned. Imagine dying in horrific pain, and never again knowing the loving warm of human contact.

Her legacy, and it is a powerful one, can be traced back to that simple statement, 'I took his hand'. That is, after all, what all caregivers do: they soothe, they listen, they support. They are the ones who go where people like Trudy Ring are reluctant to go. They're the ones who serve as buddies to people with HIV, the ones who deliver meals and accompany them to doctor's appointments, who take care of life's messy details so their friend/patient can concentrate on their health. And sometimes, their caregiving goes beyond the grave.

Arrangements to donate belongings were thwarted by organizations who refused to accept anything a person with AIDS had touched. Churches routinely refused to hold funerals or memorial services for those whose deaths they attributed to sinful behavior. In 1983, The New York State Funeral Directors Association recommended that their 11,000 members refuse to embalm anyone who appeared to have died from AIDS. It was not unusual for cities as large as Chicago to have only one funeral home that would provide services.

Since the young man's family refused to claim his body, Burks assumed responsibility for his cremation. The closest funeral home that she could find to accept him was in Pine Bluff, over forty miles away. A friend who owned a pottery store donated a chipped cookie jar for an urn. Armed with a pair of post hole diggers, she went to Files Cemetery and dug a hole in the middle of her father's grave, so the young man could rest in peace. She said a prayer for him and left.

'I took his hand' now meant something very different. Burks' family members have been buried in Files since the late 19th century. A family squabble resulted in her mother purchasing every available grave in the cemetery - 262 plots - to ensure that Burks' uncle's side of the family could never be buried there.

Burks did not fill every plot. She thinks the total is around 43. With each death, she reached out to the families, only to receive confirmation that they didn't want their sons or daughters. With each death, she conducted her own funeral service, because she couldn't convince a priest or minister to overcome their prejudices to offer prayers. Not one.

Through the years, she saw the best and worst of humanity. The mother of another dying young man called Burks to demand to know how much longer her son was going to live.

'He's ruined our lives and we don't want people up here to know (he has AIDS), so how long do you think he's going to stay here?' Like it was a punishment for her. [5]

She also saw friends and partners who stepped in to ensure that those dying were cared for with love and dignity. They became the families of choice, replacing the missing families who could not - would not - put their fears and bigotry aside, even for their child.

Eventually the deaths slowed down, the new drugs prolonging lives and making her services less necessary. Many of those who knew her then, knew what she did, are gone. Even within the AIDS community, not everyone knows her name, only that she buried people who died of AIDS.

But that simplifies all that she did. Because of being abandoned by their families, Burks often had to help the dying fill out their death certificate in advance. Why? No one else would be available later to give the information necessary. She tried, mostly in vain, to convince their families to visit.

Her goal now is to see a memorial at the cemetery, so that the remarkable story will not be forgotten. She envisions a garden, a place of contemplation, along with a weeping angel and a plaque with the names of those men, so they will never be forgotten.

In the history of the AIDS epidemic, one thing is sure: Ruth Coker Burks will never be forgotten.

Fag Hags, Divas and Moms

Closing Thoughts

"When we treat people with respect and dignity,
We reduce the impact of AIDS.
When we allow women and girls to make choices about their lives,
We reduce the impact of AIDS.
And when we give young people knowledge and information,
We empower them to protect themselves from HIV.
And we reduce the impact of AIDS.
When we no longer marginalize or criminalize people for who they are
or who they love,
We reduce the impact of AIDS."
- Victoria Beckham, UNAIDS Goodwill International Ambassador [1]

In June of 1987, fresh off a runoff election victory to represent California's 12th District, Nancy Pelosi arrived in Washington. Eager to make her first speech before the House, she asked how much time she would be allotted. "None," was the answer, which Pelosi refused to accept. She did indeed give a brief speech, as the new representative for thousands of San Franciscans affected by the epidemic, to make her priorities clear to colleagues on both sides of the aisle.

"Now we must take leadership, of course, in the crisis of AIDS. And I look forward to working with you on that." [2]

Her support of the AIDS community extended far beyond her district. Pelosi has been instrumental in legislation that included expanded access to Medicaid for people with HIV/AIDS, increased funding for the Ryan White Care (Comprehensive AIDS Resources

Emergency) Act, and passage of the Affordable Care Act (ACA). In 1992, she even convinced the National Parks Service to allow the NAMES Project to display 1,920 panels of the AIDS Quilt on the National Mall, assuring concerned bureaucrats that the grass would not be damaged.

That commitment has not wavered. Pelosi issued a statement on the 35th anniversary of the beginning of the epidemic in the US.

The story of HIV/AIDS in America is one of great tragedy, courage, and progress...As reflect on the struggles of the past 35 years, we remember the friends, family and loved ones who were lost, and rededicate ourselves to the challenges that remain. The AIDS-free generation is a dream within our grasp to achieve. In America, and abroad, let us commit to make HIV nothing more than a dark and safe memory. [3]

Rep. Maxine Waters, LA Pride Parade,
June 10, 2018 (A&U Magazine)

Another California representative, Maxine Waters, began working on AIDS as a member of the California State Assembly, before being elected to Congress in 1990. In both legislative bodies, she has taken leadership roles to fight for funding. As chair of the Congressional Black Caucus, she made AIDS a priority, working with Donna Shalala, then-Secretary of Health and Human Services, and the Clinton administration to create the Minority AIDS Initiative. That program provided funds beyond the Ryan White grants, to target at-risk minority communities around the country.

On a state level, Rep. Laura Hall of Montgomery, Alabama, became an AIDS advocate the same way many other women did: her son was diagnosed in 1988 and died three years later. She continues to be a staunch supporter of fighting the stigma that remains a barrier in the Black communities of her state. Republican opponents have gone so far as to say that AIDS was the only issue she ever talked about. Hall made no apologies.

> If you choose not to elect me because I'm very outspoken and upfront about this disease that has impacted my family, then so be it. That means I'll spend 100 percent of my time working on this issue. [4]

Women like Pelosi, Waters and Hall have led the charge in Congress and state legislatures around the country since the 1980s. They pair their personal experience and political capital to support those with the virus and those most at risk. But many of the straight women who used their celebrity in the 1980s and 1990s to bring attention to the AIDS epidemic are gone now.

Elizabeth Taylor's activism has been taken up by her family, through the work of the Elizabeth Taylor AIDS Foundation. The children, grandchildren and great-grandson of the actress aren't content to award grants to organizations around the world. They sponsor the annual AIDSWatch on Capitol Hill, drawing hundreds of HIV activists from around the US for a lobbying day to keep the heat on Congress for funding and legislation.

Princess Diana's commitment in the UK and Africa continues through her younger son, Prince Harry. He took an HIV test with singer Rihanna, a long-time AIDS activist, that was broadcast live to encourage others to learn their status. His first public appearance with then-fiancée Meghan Markle was a visit to the Terrence Higgins Trust on World AIDS Day 2017. Harry's own charity, Sentebale, supports HIV-impacted children in Lesotho and Botswana.

Colleen Dewhurst went on to become president of Actor's Equity, and in that capacity, a founder in 1987 of Equity Fights AIDS. In 1992, they merged with The Producers' Group program, Broadway Cares, to create Broadway Cares/Equity Fights AIDS. It supports not only the Actors Fund, but 450 AIDS service organizations in all 50 states, Washington, DC and Puerto Rico. Dewhurst's legacy to the AIDS community lives on through the more than $285,000,000 the group has raised for support, education and advocacy.

The Junior League of San Francisco continues their involvement today with ongoing support of the AIDS Memorial Grove, a federally-designated memorial to the AIDS epidemic in Golden Gate Park. Members of Junior League Houston, working with AIDS Foundation Houston, serve as counselors for a weeklong Camp Hope experience for children affected by HIV/AIDS. The Junior League of Montgomery (AL) partnered with Medical AIDS Outreach in 2012 to establish a food pantry for people with HIV and AIDS.

Acclaimed UK singer, songwriter and actress Beverley Knight has a large and devoted following for her work. Whether it's music inspired by her Jamaican roots or artists such as Aretha Franklin and Prince, she has moved effortlessly from gospel to R&B to soul and beyond. Onstage she's created such memorial performances as Heather Headley in *The Bodyguard* and Emmeline Pankhurst in *Sylvia*.

Beverley Knight, Antwerp, Belgium,
Sept. 26, 2005

The passion for her work is matched by her philanthropic commitment, where Knight has been a vocal advocate for the AIDS community throughout her career. The death of her close gay friend, Tyrone Jamison from AIDS in 2003, pushed her to be more involved. She has written songs inspired by him, such as "When I See You Again", and has spoken out against the stigma that prevents people from seeking the information and treatment they need. Most recently, she was named a Patron of the Terrence Higgins Trust, deepening her commitment to the organization whose services were so important to Tyrone.

Like Knight, other celebrities like Kerry Washington and Taraji P. Henson have taken on the challenge. They make expert use of social media to reach their communities, where the virus continues to ravage vulnerable populations. They reach out to young women of color via companies like MAC Cosmetics, sharing not only their love of fashion and makeup, but their message of empowering women about their health. They are passionate, vocal warriors against stigma and ignorance.

They are the public face of straight women in the AIDS community. But they simply represent the thousands of others who work in the shadows. Those women are not high-profile activists. They lack publicists. They don't document their lives on YouTube channels or Instagram. They do not receive lifetime achievement awards or have buildings named in their honor. That's not their goal. These are women whose lives are guided by a passionate belief in social justice and community involvement.

What they share with their famous sisters is a passionate desire to ensure that those who already have HIV/AIDS are treated with respect and dignity and the best care possible, to prevent future infections, to find a cure, to end this epidemic once and for all.

The women's movement has largely failed in addressing the effects of an epidemic still considered irrelevant. Despite landmark victories on reproductive health, HIV is rarely included in those advocacy efforts. In doing so, a crisis that disproportionately affects poor women and women of color has been ignored.

These mostly anonymous women have put their bodies on the line, sometimes literally, to fight for the rights of people with HIV/AIDS. They have delivered meals, cared for, and housed people who were abandoned by their birth families. They have comforted the living and buried the dead. They have raised money and awareness and given hope to those in despair. They have celebrated successes and mourned too many lives cut short by a virus and stigma. And their efforts have largely gone unrecognized.

This book has offered an overview of the HIV community and its uneasy relationship with straight women, even as these outsiders have persisted to achieve great strides for people with AIDS. It remains an area of women's history that has been consistently ignored. Hopefully, it begins the process of reclaiming the role of straight women during the ongoing epidemic - thereby ensuring a greater welcome in the future to those women who are drawn to make a difference for everyone infected or affected by AIDS.

The story of straight women in the AIDS movement is not over. It has, in many ways, been untold. Here and there, small efforts have been made to preserve those stories. The ACT UP Oral History Project includes a few straight women who sat down to be interviewed about their involvement. Australian Dirk Hoult created *We Were There*, a verbatim play based on interviews with women in the AIDS community. A few websites and magazines specific to the AIDS community feature straight allies, including many of the women here. Hopefully this book will serve as an incentive for other straight women who have worked and continue to work in the HIV/AIDS community to come forward with their own stories.

When I first approached them for this project, too many of the women interviewed initially objected, "Why would anyone care about my story?" Their modest or skeptical attitudes reaffirmed the need for this book. I found myself reminding them of their pioneer status, of their value to advocacy work, of the fact that recognition for their contribution is long overdue. Moreover, their work is part of a larger story in the epidemic: one of rare and crucial compassion, sacrifice, commitment and love.

It's time for straight women in the AIDS movement to come out of the closet and share the spotlight they so richly deserve. Their stories have only begun to be told.

Fag Hags, Divas and Moms

Acknowledgements

They say writing is a solitary endeavor and it is. But a book like this cannot be written without the generosity of others. When I began this journey in September 2015, I wasn't sure if anyone thought it was an important topic. I was humbled time and again by the willingness of people to trust me with their stories on this journey. There are many people to thank:

I have to begin with Terri Wilder, whose "The Women of ACT UP/NY: Fight Back! Fight AIDS!" panel at the New York Public Library in 2014 sparked the idea for this book. Little did I know it would change my life.

My editor, Jay Blotcher, who guided me in ways that were sometimes painfully honest, but always right on target. I could not have done this without him.

The New York Foundation for the Arts for granting this project fiscal sponsorship. The Department of Cultural Affairs and Special Events of the City of Chicago, for their financial support. A special thanks to the people who supported my crowdfunding efforts, including Donna Andrews, David Beckwith, Ruth Burich, Eileen Dreyer, Nancy Duncan, Thomas Egan, James Eigo, Shelly Immel, Vivian Imperiale, Julie Johnson, Mark S. King, Sarah Kelly, Kathleen Pooler, Amy Raspatello, Garth Reese, Lynn McCollum Staley, Peter Staley, Nancy Taylor and Shirley Utterback-Wilson.

A shout-out to those who directly helped with research, including the always helpful staff at the Edgebrook branch of Chicago Public Library. I'm grateful to the research librarians at the University of Chicago Regenstein Library as well as those at the New York Public Library (Stephen A. Scharzman Building and the Performing Arts, Dorothy & Lewis B. Cullman Center branches). The generosity of the women of the Association of Junior Leagues International office in New York and the Junior League of San Francisco in sharing their archives is deeply appreciated.

The owners of Women & Children First bookstore in Chicago and Bureau of General Services-Queer Division in New York enthusiastically supported the idea of this book from the start.

Dozens of friends and strangers answered my social media calls for assistance with enthusiasm, humor and generosity. Their support, more than anything, convinced me that these women deserved to be recognized.

My beta readers – David Beckwith, Ann Mitchell Smith, Lawrence Arancio, Maia Gilman and Kathleen Pooler – encouraged and challenged me when I needed it.

He may not think he deserves any credit, but my neurologist, Dr. Elliot Roth, made this book possible. It took several years after my 2009 concussion to find a doctor who took me seriously and could help me navigate the challenges of post-concussive syndrome. But the day I walked into the Shirley Ryan Ability Lab, I knew I'd finally found the support I needed. Without his guidance and encouragement, this book would not have been written.

As always, much gratitude to my family for their patience. This was a book with many roadblocks: a broken writing hand, three computers that gave me too many headaches, my mother's death. Mom felt guilty that her final illness took me away from my work. But it is a better book because of her unwavering love and belief in me.

Finally, and most important, straight women in the AIDS community. I thank you all from the bottom of my heart. You shared your stories and personal photos with me, often with a box of Kleenex between us. Not all of you made it into this book, but your stories will still be shared in other ways. I hope that your openness will inspire other women to tell their stories, too.

Notes

Preface
1. Invocation (unattributed), US Conference on AIDS, Sept. 18, 2015.
2. Terri Wilder, personal interview, May 22, 2017.

Introduction
1. Welcome letter from Colleen Dewhurst, program for Equity Fights AIDS benefit performance of *A Chorus Line*, April 8, 1990.
2. Colleen Dewhurst with Tom Viola, *Colleen Dewhurst: Her Autobiography*, (New York: Scribner, 2002) p. 322.
3. *Colleen Dewhurst: Her Autobiography*, p. 323-324.
4. HIV in Ireland study, HIVIreland.ie, Sept. 28, 2017.
5. Cynthia O'Neal, *Talk Softly: A Memoir* (New York: Seven Stories press, 2010), p. 116.
6. Jih-Fei Cheng, *How to Survive: AIDS and Afterlife in Public*, (New York: Feminist Press). p. 78.

The Volunteers
1. Marjorie J. Hill, "Joan Tisch: Face to Face with a Living Legend", GMHC.org, March 13, 2011.
2. Terri Wilder personal interview, May 22, 2017.
3. Terri Wilder personal interview.

The Educators
1. Colin Deppen, "Don't think AIDS happens to people like you? Neither did she", PennLive.com, April 26, 2016.
2. Rosa E. Martinez-Colón, "Women's History Month", victorianoe.com, March 15, 2016.
3. Rosa E. Martinez-Colón.
4. Rosa E. Martinez-Colón, personal correspondence to author.
5. "Making One Final Step: It Is Time", theredpumpproject.com, Aug. 1, 2018.

6.   Heather Arculeo, "Who Am I?" A Woman's Voice, *A&U Magazine*, May 11, 2015.

7.   Heather Arculeo.

8.   Naomi Pfefferman, "A Young Woman Talks Life with HIV," etaf.org, May 25, 2016.

9.   Sarah Hashmall, "Positive Organizing Shero: Martha Cameron," AIDSUnited.org, March 15, 2017.

10.   Nancy Duncan, "Women's History Month", victorianoe.com, March 8, 2016.

11.   Nancy Duncan personal interview, Aug. 17, 2017.

12.   Nancy Duncan personal correspondence to author.

13.   Angela McLaurin, *Chicago Tribune* obituary, May 19, 2016.

14.   Colin Deppen.

15.   Iris de la Cruz, "Ode to the Sisterhood", *Kool AIDS on Ice*, 1989.

The Nonprofit Executives

1.   Sarah Toce, "Remembering Project Open Hand Founder Ruth Brinker", *Windy City Times*, Jan. 11, 2012.

2.   Krishna Stone, personal interview, March 30, 2017.

3.   Krishna Stone interview.

4.   Ingrid Floyd personal interview, May 25, 2017.

5.   Ingrid Floyd personal interview.

6.   Carol D. Marsh, *Nowhere Else I Want to Be*, (San Francisco: Inkshares, Inc., 2017) p. 21.

7.   Carol D. Marsh, pg. 27.

8.   Carol D. Marsh, pg. 36.

9.   Krishna Stone personal interview.

The Medical Establishment and Their Patients

1.   Ronald Bayer and Gerald M. Oppenheimer, *AIDS Doctors: Voices from the Epidemic*, (New York: Oxford University Press, 2000) p. 82.

2.   Bayer and Oppenheimer, p. 88.

3.   Bayer and Oppenheimer, p. 100.

4.   Kathleen Pooler, "Women's History Month", victorianoe.com, March 8, 2017.

5.   Bayer and Oppenheimer, p. 83.

6.   Bayer and Oppenheimer, p. 261.

7.   Bayer and Oppenheimer, p. 56.

8.   Mary Jordan, "Women and HIV", *Positively Aware*, January, 1992.

9.   The Denver Principles, 1983.

10.   Bayer and Oppenheimer, p. 179.

The Researchers

1. Unnamed senior staff member to Francoise Barré-Sinoussi, Pasteur Institute, 1975.

2. Patrick Strudwick, "In Conversation with...Francoise Barré-Sinoussi", MosaicScience.com, May 27, 2014.

3. Patrick Strudwick.

4. Patrick Strudwick.

5. Esther Landhuis and Mark Jones, "Mathilde Krim's Life of Causes", Medium.com, Dec. 8, 2015.

6. Landhuis and Jones.

7. Marjorie Ingall, "Farewell to a longtime AIDS activist", Tablet Magazine, Jan. 16, 2018.

8. Peter Staley, personal correspondence with author, Jan. 13, 2019.

9. Leah Samuel, "5 Important Ways Henrietta Lacks changed medical science", STAT, 4/14/17.

The Spiritual Community

1. Trudy James, *In the Beginning: AIDS Spirituality and CareTeams*, (Seattle, WA: Multifaith Works Press, 2007), p. 9.

2. Trudy James, p. 9.

3. Trudy James, p. 50.

4. Cynthia O'Neal, *Talk Softly: A Memoir*, New York: Seven Stories Press, 2010, p. 19.

5. Cynthia O'Neal, p. 215.

6. Sheri Lewis, "In Defense of Louise Hay", body.com, Nov. 14, 2017.

The Moms

1. Anne King, "What it feels like for a mom", MyFabulousDisease.com, April 29, 2010.

2. Regan Hofmann, *I Have Something to Tell You*, New York: Atria Books, 2013, p. 42.

3. Kate Harmon, "The AIDS Memorial Quilt: A Conversation with Mother Arlene Bubb", FamilyFirstHealth.org, May 24, 2016.

4. Editorial, *The (Raleigh) News & Observer*, June 2, 1995.

5. Patsy Clarke and Eloise Vaughn, with Nicole Brodeur, *Keep Singing: Two Mothers, Two Sons, and Their Fight Against Jesse Helms*, Los Angeles: Alyson Publications, 2001, p. 77-78.

6. "Rev. Willie T. Barrow, 'Little Warrior' was civil rights leader, mentor," *Chicago Sun Times*, June 24, 2016.

7. Lori Cannon, "Views: Paying Tribute to Andrew Patner", *Windy City Times*, April 1, 2015.

8. Statement by Jeanne Manford, NAMES Project AIDS Memorial Quilt display, Washington, DC, Oct. 10, 1992.

9. Test Positive Aware Network website.

10. Testimony by Louise Ray, Committee to Study HIV transmission through blood products, US Dept. of Commerce, September 12, 1994.

11. Jeanne White-Ginder, dedication of the Hemophilia Memorial Circle, AIDS Memorial Grove, San Francisco, Sept. 16, 2017.

12. Brent Nicholson Earle personal interview, July 28, 2018.

13. Brent Nicholson Earle personal interview.

14. 1992 Democratic Party Platform.

15. 1992 Republican Party Platform.

16. Mary Fisher, Speech to 1992 Republican National Convention.

17. Kate Harmon.

18. Tommy Tomlinson, "The last time she crossed paths with Helms, sympathy stirred," *The Charlotte Observer*, July 5, 2008.

The Divas
1. Elizabeth Taylor, Senate testimony on Ryan White funding, 1990.

2. Nancy Collins, "Liz's AIDS Odyssey", *Vanity Fair*, November, 1992.

3. M.G. Lord, *The Accidental Feminist: How Elizabeth Taylor Raised Our Consciousness and We Were Too Distracted by Her Beauty to Notice*, New York: Walker Books, 2013, p. 162.

4. M.G. Lord, p. 160.

5. *Diana, Our Mother: Her Life and Legacy*, ITV/HBO, July 24, 2017.

6. Randy Shilts, *And the Band Played On*, New York: St. Martin's Griffin, 2007, p 331.

7. Dann Dulin, "In Bed with Carrie Fisher", *A&U Magazine*, April, 1998.

8. Dann Dulin, "Melissa Rivers: Cover Story", *A&U Magazine*, April, 2018.

9. God's Love We Deliver website.

10. Sean Black, "Cover Story: Donna Mills", *A&U Magazine*, April, 2015.

11. Dan Dulin, "Rita Moreno: Cover Story", *A&U Magazine*, Oct. 26, 2013.

12. "The A-List Interview: Kerry Washington", *The Advocate*, Oct. 31, 2013.

13. Black AIDS Institute website.

14. Rae Lewis-Thornton, personal correspondence with author.

The Fag Hags
1. JD Davids, "Nora Burns on *David's Friend*, Her One-Woman Show on AIDS, Love, Loss and Great Old Disco", thebody.com, Jan 18, 2017.

2. Yolo Akili Robinson, "Gay Men's Sexism and Women's Bodies", *The Good Men Project*, Nov. 4, 2012.

3. Trudy Ring, "AIDS: The Remembering", *Windy City Times*, October 19, 2011.

4. Ilene Shaw personal interview, May 31, 2017.

5. Ilene Shaw personal interview.

6. Nora Burns, Program notes, *David's Friend*.

7. David Olmsted, "The Writer as Witness: Novelist Julia Glass Talks to Mark Olmsted about AIDS, Loss & the Consolation of Words", *A&U Magazine*, Nov. 25, 2017.

The Fictional Women

1. Armistead Maupin, *Michael Tolliver Lives*, New York: Harper Collins, 2007, p. 269.

2. Tom Hayes, "Emmerdale Team Talks About Val Testing HIV-Positive", beyondpositive.org, Feb. 19, 2014.

3. Tom Hayes.

4. Linda Bloodworth-Thomason, *Designing Women*, "All the Right People", Oct. 5, 1987.

5. "Gloria Reuben recalls HIV-positive role on ER", CTVNews.ca, March, 11, 2009.

6. Jim Colucci, *Golden Girls Forever: An Unauthorized Look Behind the Lanai*, New York: Harper Design, 2016, p. 223.

7. Larry Kramer, *The Normal Heart*, p. 103.

8. Larry Kramer, p. 103-4.

9. Larry Kramer, p. 104.

10. Armistead Maupin, *Mary Ann in Autumn*, New York: Harper Perennial, 2011, p. 1.

11. Rebecca Makkai, *The Great Believers*, New York: Viking, 2018, p. 269.

12. Rebecca Makkai, p.283.

The Activists

1. Emma Thompson, "AIDS: Ask Emma Thompson", BBC interview, Nov. 25, 2001.

2. Benita Roth, *The Life and Death of ACT UP/LA: AIDS Activism in Los Angeles from the 1980s to the 2000s*, New York: Cambridge University Press, 2017, pg. 85-86.

3. Nanette Kazaoka, ACT UP/NY Oral History Project, January 15, 2014.

4. Nanette Kazaoka.

5. Chael Needle, "I Want to See U Be Brave", *A&U Magazine*, December 5, 2015.

6. Jim Eigo, The Atlanta principles, actupny.com, 2014.

7. Iris De La Cruz, Kool AIDS on Ice, IrisHouse.org, 1989.

The Artists

1. Woody Hochswender, "AIDS and the Fashion World: Industry Fears for Its Health", New York Times, Feb. 11, 1990.

2. Estate Project for Artists with AIDS Project, Alliance for the Arts, 1992.

3. Tory Dent, "Many Rivers to Cross," When Silence Equals, (New York: Persea Books, 1993), p. 68.

4. Adrienne Rich, "Tory Dent's Poetry on Life with AIDS", npr.com, January 3, 2006.
5. Valerie Lau-Kee Lai personal interview, October 27, 2016.
6. Valerie Lau-Kee Lai.
7. Valerie Lau-Kee Lai.
8. Denise Roberts Hurlin personal interview, October 27, 2016.

The Caregivers
1. Jennifer Miller, "Struggling with AIDS: A Sister's Perspective", *Positively Aware*, March 1992
2. Jennifer Miller.
3. Dann Dulin, "Ruth Coker Burks: Advocate", *A&U Magazine*, Dec. 22, 2017.
4. Dann Dulin.
5. Dann Dulin.

Closing Thoughts
1. Victoria Beckham, remarks to UNAIDS (?), Nov. 23, 2018.
2. Nancy Pelosi, address to the House of Representatives, June 9, 1987.
3. Nancy Pelosi, statement on 35th Anniversary of HIV/AIDS in America, June 6, 2016.
4. Laura Hall, "In the Capital – Voices from the Political Arena", *AIDS in Blackface*, Black AIDS Institute, 2013.

Index

Fag Hags, Divas and Moms

Permissions

Permissions

WHAT WOMEN WANT(c)1990, Daniel Sotomayor, Artist. Original artwork, Ink on Vellum, Sotomayor Collection. Lori F. Dannon, Owner. Documentation and Curation Courtesy of The Legacy Project

"ACT UP Women's Caucus direct action, City Hall, Chicago, April, 1990" photo by Linda Miller. Originally published in "The Thrill is Gone: confessions of a former AIDS activist", essay by Mary Patten in *The Passionate Camera*. Permission granted by Mary Patten.

Fag Hags, Divas and Moms

About the Author

Victoria Noe is an award-winning author, speaker and activist.

In 2006, she promised a dying friend that she would write a book about people grieving their friends. That book turned into the *Friend Grief* series, six small nonfiction collections of stories from people whose lives changed after their friends died. With these books, she filled a gap in grief resources.

Noe's freelance work has appeared in *Chicago Tribune, Huffington Post, Windy City Times* and a variety of writing and HIV-related websites. Her essay, "Long-Term Survivor" won the 2015 Christopher Hewitt Award for Creative Nonfiction from *A&U Magazine*. A sought-after speaker, she has presented at such venues as The Muse and the Marketplace, Mt. Sinai Medical Center HIV rounds, and public libraries around the Midwest.

Her work in the AIDS community in Chicago began in the mid-1980s as a volunteer, then as a fundraiser for a variety of AIDS-service organization until 1994. After a long break, she returned as a writer and advocate in 2011. Her main interests are sharing stories of women in the AIDS community and supporting the needs of long-term survivors.

Noe holds bachelor's and master's degrees in Speech and Dramatic Art from the University of Iowa, and uses her experience as a stage manager and director to help shy authors overcome their fear of public speaking.

She is a member of the Alliance of Independent Authors, Chicago Writers Association and ACT UP/NY. A St. Louis native, she remains a loyal Cardinals fan despite living in Chicago, married to a Cubs fan.

Connect with Victoria:

www.victorianoe.com

victoria@victorianoe.com

Twitter.com/Victoria_Noe

Facebook.com/VictoriaNoeAuthor

Instagram.com/victorianoe1131

Books by Victoria Noe

Friend Grief and Men: Defying Stereotypes

Friend Grief in the Workplace: More Than an Empty Cubicle

Friend Grief and the Military: Band of Friends

Friend Grief and 9/11: The Forgotten Mourners

Friend Grief and AIDS: Thirty Years of Burying Our Friends

*Friend Grief and Anger: When Your Friend Dies and
No One Gives a Damn*

Fag Hags, Divas and Moms

CPSIA information can be obtained
at www.ICGtesting.com
Printed in the USA
LVHW081724080819
626995LV00015B/1289/P